• Cooking for Today •

SIMPLE CHINESE RECIPES

• Cooking for Today •

SIMPLE
CHINESE
RECIPES

DEH-TA HSIUNG　　　WENDY LEE

WHITECAP BOOKS

This edition published in 1997 by:
Whitecap Books Ltd.
351 Lynn Avenue
North Vancouver
BC V7J 2C4

ISBN 1-55110-703-1

Produced by Haldane Mason, London

Printed in Italy

Photographs on pages 12, 24, 32, 62 and 72 reproduced by
permission of Tony Stone Images; on pages 84, 96, 108, 124, 140,
156, 168, 178, 190 and 208 reproduced by permission of ZEFA
Picture Library (UK) Ltd.

Note:
*Cup measurements in this book are for American cups. Tablespoons are
assumed to be 15ml. Unless otherwise stated, milk is assumed to be full-
fat, eggs are standard size 2 and pepper is freshly ground black pepper.*

Contents

SIMPLE
Chinese
RECIPES

The cuisine of China is varied and diverse.
Each region has different specialities, such as
the hot, spicy dishes of the Szechuan region,
and the aromatic crispy duck from Beijing. In
Chinese cuisine, the emphasis is on a balance
of flavors, aromas, textures and colors in
each meal. Many dishes are simple to
prepare, and all are delicious.

This colorful and comprehensive selection of
recipes from the different regions of China
provides a glorious range of exotic dishes,
with step-by-step instructions showing how
to prepare each one. Over the following
pages, discover how to create these elegant
and delicious dishes in your own kitchen
to serve as exciting everyday meals or
as special-occasion dinners to delight
your guests.

1

CANTONESE
COOKING

CHAPTER ONE

Appetizers

A number of dishes in Cantonese cooking are served as an appetizer – just like hors d'oeuvres in the West. One of the advantages of these dishes is that they are generally prepared and cooked well in advance – hours or even days before serving. Also, almost all the dishes selected here are ideal for a buffet-style meal or as party food.

Instead of serving different appetizers individually, try serving a small portion of each together as an assorted hors d'oeuvres. Select a minimum of three or four different items: Crispy Egg Rolls, Butterfly Shrimp, Barbecue Spareribs, Barbecue Pork (Char Siu), and so on.

Other dishes from the Main Course section that can be served as a part of the appetizer are Sweet and Sour Shrimp, Lemon Chicken, and Baked Crab with Ginger and Scallions. Remember not to have more than one of the same type of food – the ingredients should be chosen for their harmony and balance in color, aroma, flavor and texture.

Opposite: A Chinese cook at an open-air stall in Xinjiang province. Wayside stalls selling takeout food are a common sight all over China, offering wontons, spare ribs, shrimp, egg rolls and other tasty snacks for hungry workers.

STEP 3

STEP 4

STEP 5

STEP 6

CRISPY VEGETARIAN EGG ROLLS

For a non-vegetarian version, just replace mushrooms with chicken or pork, and the carrots with shrimp.

MAKES 12 ROLLS

2 cups fresh bean sprouts, washed
   and drained
1-2 scallions
1 medium carrot
$^1/_3$ cup canned sliced bamboo shoots, rinsed
   and drained
1 cup mushrooms
2–3 tbsp vegetable oil, plus oil for
   deep-frying
$^1/_2$ tsp salt
$^1/_2$ tsp sugar
1 tbsp light soy sauce
1 tsp Chinese rice wine or dry sherry
12 egg roll skins, defrosted if frozen
1 tbsp cornstarch paste (see page 231)
flour for dusting
vegetable oil for deep-frying

1 Cut all the vegetables into thin shreds roughly the same size and shape as the bean sprouts.

2 Heat the oil in a preheated wok and stir-fry the vegetables for about 1 minute. Add the salt, sugar, soy sauce and wine and continue stirring for 1½–2 minutes. Remove the vegetables from the wok with a slotted spoon and place in a bowl. Drain off the excess liquid then let cool.

3 To make the egg rolls, place about 2 tablespoons of the vegetables one-third of the way down on an egg roll skin, with the triangle pointing away from you.

4 Lift the lower flap over the filling and fold in one end.

5 Roll once and fold in the other end to completely enclose the filling.

6 Roll once more, brush the upper edge with a little cornstarch paste, and roll into a neat package. Lightly dust a tray with flour and place the egg roll with the flap-side down. Make the remaining egg rolls the same.

7 Heat the oil in a preheated wok or deep-fryer until smoking, then reduce the heat to low and deep-fry the egg rolls in batches for 2–3 minutes or until golden and crispy. Remove with a slotted spoon and drain on paper towels. Serve hot with a dipping sauce, such as soy sauce, sweet and sour sauce or chili sauce, which you can buy at the supermarket.

BUTTERFLY SHRIMP

Use unpeeled raw jumbo or tiger shrimp which are about 3–4 inches long.

STEP 1

STEP 1

STEP 3

STEP 3

SERVES 4

12 raw jumbo or tiger shrimp in their shells
2 tbsp light soy sauce
1 tbsp Chinese rice wine or dry sherry
1 tbsp cornstarch
2 eggs, lightly beaten
8–10 tbsp bread crumbs
vegetable oil for deep-frying
salt and pepper
shredded lettuce leaves, to serve
chopped scallions, to garnish

1 Peel and devein the shrimp but leave the tails on. Split them in half from the underbelly about halfway along, leaving the tails firmly attached.

2 Mix together the salt, pepper, soy sauce, wine and cornstarch in a bowl, add the shrimp and turn to coat. Let marinate for 10–15 minutes.

3 Heat the oil in a preheated wok. Pick up each shrimp by the tail, dip it in the beaten egg then roll it in the bread crumbs to coat well.

4 Deep-fry the shrimp in batches until golden brown. Remove them with a slotted spoon and drain on paper towels.

5 To serve, arrange the shrimp neatly on a bed of lettuce leaves and garnish with scallions, either raw or soaked for about 30 seconds in hot oil.

VARIATIONS

Butterfly shrimp may also be served on a bed of crispy seaweed (see page 88). This classic Chinese accompaniment provides the perfect foil for the luscious shrimp. Dried seaweed can be bought in packages from Oriental food stores and supermarkets. Follow the instructions on the package to prepare it.

TO DEVEIN LARGE SHRIMP

First remove the shell. Make a shallow cut about three-quarters of the way along the back of each shrimp, then pull out and discard the black intestinal vein.

STEP 1

STEP 2

STEP 3

STEP 4

LETTUCE-WRAPPED GROUND MEAT

The original version of this recipe uses quail or pigeon meat.
Serve the ground meat and lettuce leaves on separate dishes;
each guest then wraps his or her own parcel.

SERVES 4

1¹/₂ cups ground pork or chicken
1 tbsp finely chopped Chinese mushrooms
1 tbsp finely chopped water chestnuts
salt and pepper
pinch sugar
1 tsp light soy sauce
1 tsp Chinese rice wine or dry sherry
1 tsp cornstarch
2–3 tbsp vegetable oil
¹/₂ tsp finely chopped gingerroot
1 tsp finely chopped scallions
1 tbsp finely chopped Szechuan preserved
  vegetables (optional)
1 tbsp oyster sauce
a few drops sesame oil
8 crisp lettuce leaves, to serve

1 Mix the ground meat with the mushrooms, water chestnuts, salt, pepper, sugar, soy sauce, wine and cornstarch.

2 Heat the oil in a preheated wok or skillet. Add the ginger and scallions followed by the meat. Stir-fry for 1 minute.

3 Add the Szechuan preserved vegetables and continue stirring for 1 more minute. Add the oyster sauce and

sesame oil, blend well and cook for 1 more minute. Remove to a warmed serving dish.

4 To serve: place 2–3 tablespoons of the mixture on a lettuce leaf and roll it up tightly to form a small parcel. Eat with your fingers.

SZECHUAN PRESERVED VEGETABLES

These pickled mustard roots are hot and salty, with a peppery flavor, and are often used to intensify the spiciness of a dish. Once opened, store in the refrigerator in a tightly sealed jar.

STEP 1

STEP 2

STEP 3

STEP 4

BARBECUE SPARERIBS

This is a simplified version of the half saddle of pork ribs seen hanging in the windows of Cantonese restaurants. Use the specially small, thin ribs known as finger ribs.

SERVES 4
OVEN: 450°F; THEN 400°F

1 lb pork finger spareribs
1 tbsp sugar
1 tbsp light soy sauce
1 tbsp dark soy sauce
3 tbsp hoi-sin sauce
1 tbsp rice wine or dry sherry
4–5 tbsp water or Chinese Stock (see page 230)
mild chili sauce, to dip
cilantro leaves, to garnish

1 Trim off any excess fat from the ribs and cut into pieces. Mix the ribs with the sugar, light and dark soy sauces, hoi-sin sauce and wine in a baking dish, and marinate for 2–3 hours.

2 Add the water or stock to the ribs and spread them out in the dish. Roast in a preheated hot oven for 15 minutes.

3 Turn the ribs over, lower the heat and continue roasting for 30–35 minutes longer.

4 To serve, chop each rib into 3–4 small, bite-sized pieces with a large knife or Chinese cleaver and arrange on a serving dish. Pour the sauce from the baking dish over them, garnish with cilantro leaves, and serve with chili sauce as a dip.

HOI-SIN SAUCE

This sweet, thick sauce is made from soybean flour, soy beans, vinegar, sesame seed oil, chili, sugar, salt, garlic and spices. It is sold in cans and jars; if you buy it in a can, store it in a glass bottle in the refrigerator once opened, where it will keep for several months. It is ideal for use in marinades and as a dip or condiment for many Chinese dishes.

SPARERIBS

Ask your local butcher to cut some if you can't find the right size of ribs in the supermarket. Don't throw away any trimmings from the ribs – they can be used for soup or stock.

STEP 1

STEP 2

STEP 4

STEP 5

BARBECUE PORK (CHAR SIU)

Also called honey-roasted pork, these are the strips of reddish meat sometimes seen hanging in the windows of Cantonese restaurants.

SERVES 4
OVEN: 425°F; THEN 350°F

1 lb pork tenderloin
²/₃ cup boiling water
1 tbsp honey, dissolved with a little hot
    water
shredded lettuce, to serve

MARINADE:
1 tbsp sugar
1 tbsp crushed yellow bean sauce
1 tbsp light soy sauce
1 tbsp hoi-sin sauce
1 tbsp oyster sauce
½ tsp chili sauce
1 tbsp brandy or rum
1 tsp sesame oil

1 Cut the pork into strips about 1 inch thick and 7–8 inches long and place in a large shallow dish. Add the marinade ingredients and turn the pork in the mixture until well coated. Cover and let marinate for at least 3–4 hours, turning occasionally.

2 Remove the pork strips from the dish with a slotted spoon, reserving the marinade. Arrange the pork strips on a rack over a baking pan. Place the pan in the preheated oven and pour in the boiling water. Roast for about 10–15 minutes.

3 Lower the oven temperature. Baste the pork strips with the reserved marinade and turn. Roast for a further 10 minutes.

4 Remove the pork from the oven, brush with the honey syrup, and lightly brown under a medium-hot broiler for 3–4 minutes, turning them over once or twice.

5 To serve, let the pork cool slightly before cutting it. Cut across the grain into thin slices and arrange on a bed of shredded lettuce. Make a sauce by boiling the marinade and the drippings in the baking pan for a few minutes, strain and pour over the pork.

CHAPTER TWO

Soups

Soup is not normally served as a separate course in China, except at
formal occasions and banquets – and then it usually
appears towards the end of the meal.

At an everyday meal in Chinese homes, a simply made soup, almost
always a clear broth in which a small amount of thinly sliced
or shredded vegetables and/or meat have been poached quickly,
is served with the other dishes in the meal.

If a good stock is not available, as is often the case in Chinese
homes, a Chinese housewife would just stir-fry the ingredients first
in a little oil, then add water and seasonings (salt, soy sauce or
monosodium glutamate) to make an instant soup fit for the gods!

If you use a chicken bouillon cube, remember to reduce the
amount of seasonings in the recipes, since most commercially-made
bouillon cubes are fairly salty and spicy. It is always worth
making your own Chinese Stock (see page 230)
if you have the time.

Opposite: *Father and son enjoy
a bowl of soup with wontons in
a Shanghai restaurant. In
China soup is usually served
with other dishes as part of a
meal, not a separate course as
in the West.*

CORN & CRAB-MEAT SOUP

You must use creamed corn for this soup, which originated in America.
Chicken can be used instead of the crab meat, if preferred.

STEP 1

SERVES 4

½ cup crab meat
¼ tsp finely chopped gingerroot
2 egg whites
2 tbsp milk
1 tbsp cornstarch paste (see page 231)
2 ½ cups Chinese Stock (see page 230)
8-oz can creamed corn
salt and pepper
finely chopped scallions, to garnish

STEP 2

1 Flake the crab meat (or coarsely chop the chicken breast) and mix with the ginger.

2 Beat the egg whites until frothy, add the milk and cornstarch paste and beat again until smooth. Blend in the crab or chicken.

3 In a wok or large skillet, bring the stock to a boil, add the creamed corn and bring back to a boil.

4 Stir in the crab meat or chicken pieces and egg-white mixture, adjust the seasoning and stir gently until the mixture is well blended. Serve hot, garnished with chopped scallions.

CHOOSING CRAB

Always buy the freshest possible crab; fresh is best, though frozen or canned will work for this recipe. The delicate, sweet flavor of crab diminishes quickly: this is why many Chinese cooks make a point of buying live crab.

STEP 3

CREAMED CORN

Although corn is not unknown in Asia today, it really is a Western food by tradition. Be sure to use proper creamed corn for this soup, as it has quite a different texture from the more usual corn kernels. Creamed corn has a thick, slightly mushy consistency, making a thick, creamy soup.

STEP 4

STEP 1

STEP 2

STEP 3

STEP 5

SEAFOOD & TOFU SOUP

Use shrimp, squid or scallops, or a combination of all three.

SERVES 4

*1¹/₂ cups seafood, such as peeled shrimp,
   squid or scallops, defrosted if frozen
¹/₂ egg white, lightly beaten
1 tbsp cornstarch paste (see page 231)
1 cake tofu
3 cups Chinese Stock (see page 230)
1 tbsp light soy sauce
salt and pepper
fresh cilantro leaves, to garnish*

1 Small shrimp can be left whole;
larger ones should be cut into
smaller pieces; cut the squid and scallops
into small pieces.

2 If raw, mix the shrimp and scallops
with the egg white and cornstarch
paste to prevent them from becoming
tough when they are cooked.

3 Cut the cake of tofu into about 24
small cubes.

4 Bring the stock to a rolling boil.
Add the tofu and soy sauce, bring
back to a boil and simmer for 1 minute.

5 Stir in the seafood, raw pieces first,
pre-cooked ones last. Bring back to
a boil and simmer for just 1 minute.

Adjust the seasoning and serve
garnished with fresh cilantro leaves, if
liked.

FRESH CILANTRO

The musky, sharp scent and flavor of fresh
cilantro is truly distinctive. When buying it
fresh, look for bright green, unwilted
leaves. To store it, wash and dry the
leaves and leave them on the stem. Wrap
the leaves in damp paper towels and keep
them in a plastic bag in the refrigerator.

TOFU

Tofu, also known as bean curd, is an
almost tasteless substance made from
crushed yellow soy beans which are
very high in protein. It is widely available
in supermarkets, and Oriental and health-
food stores. It is sold in cakes about
3 inches square.

STEP 1

STEP 2

STEP 3

STEP 4

MIXED VEGETABLE SOUP

Select three or four of the suggested vegetables for this soup: the Chinese like to blend different colors, flavors and textures in order to create harmony as well as contrast.

SERVES 4

about ¹/₂–1 cup each of mushrooms, carrots, asparagus, snow peas, bamboo shoots, baby corn, English cucumber, tomatoes, spinach, lettuce, Chinese leaves, tofu, etc.
2 ¹/₂ cups Chinese Stock (see page 230)
1 tbsp light soy sauce
a few drops sesame oil (optional)
salt and pepper
finely chopped scallions, to garnish

1 Cut your selection of vegetables into roughly uniform shapes (slices, shreds or cubes) and sizes.

2 Bring the stock to a rolling boil in a wok and add the vegetables, bearing in mind that some require a longer cooking time than others: add carrots and baby corn first, cook for 2 minutes, then add asparagus, mushrooms, Chinese leaves, tofu and cook for another minute.

3 Add spinach, lettuce, watercress, cucumber and tomato last. Stir and bring the soup back to a boil.

4 Add soy sauce and the sesame oil, and adjust the seasoning. Serve hot, garnished with scallions.

SESAME OIL

Sesame oil is a low-saturate oil widely used for its nutty, aromatic flavor. This rich-flavored oil is made from toasted sesame seeds and used as a seasoning, not as a cooking oil. Thick and dark, it burns easily, so it should be added at the last moment, just before serving. It makes a wonderful dressing for salads when diluted with other vegetable oils. A few drops are often added to soups and other dishes just before serving – it can often be seen floating on the surface, as in the photograph opposite.

CHAPTER THREE

Main Course Dishes

The main course dishes in a conventional Chinese meal are usually stir-fried or braised. Certain dishes may require a longer cooking time and, strictly speaking, belong to a separate course – known as the principal dish – and should be served independently.

Stir-frying meat and fish dishes have become very popular in Western kitchens in recent years. This is because these dishes are comparatively simple and easy to prepare and cook, as well as being economical, delicious and healthy. Basically, the ingredients are cut into small, thin slices or shreds, then tossed and stirred in hot oil over high heat for a very short time. Thus the natural flavors, as well as the subtle textures, of the ingredients are preserved. When correctly done, the meats (which include fish and poultry) should be tender and juicy, and the vegetables crisp and bright – overcooking will render the food into a tasteless soggy mess.

Opposite: *Work is finished for the day, and a cook in XinJiang sells noodles for the evening meal. It takes years to learn the art of making noodles and the products of specialist noodle-makers are greatly sought after.*

STEP 1

STEP 2

STEP 3

STEP 4

SWEET & SOUR SHRIMP

Use raw shrimp if possible; ready-cooked ones can be added to the sauce without the initial deep-frying (step 2).

SERVES 4

*1¹/₃–2 cups raw jumbo or tiger shrimp in
   their shells
vegetable oil for deep-frying
fresh cilantro leaves, to garnish*

*SAUCE:
1 tbsp vegetable oil
2 tsp finely chopped scallions
1 tsp finely chopped gingerroot
1 tbsp light soy sauce
2 tbsp sugar
3 tbsp rice vinegar
1 tsp Chinese rice wine or dry sherry
¹/₂ cup Chinese Stock (see page 230) or
   water
1 tbsp cornstarch paste (see page 231)
a few drops sesame oil
cilantro leaves, to garnish*

1 Remove the legs from the shrimp but leave the body shells.

2 Heat the oil in a preheated wok. Deep-fry the shrimp in the hot oil for about 45–50 seconds, or until they become bright orange. Remove with a slotted spoon and drain well on paper towels.

3 To make the sauce, heat the oil in a preheated wok and add the scallions and ginger, followed by the seasonings, sugar and stock or water. Bring to a boil.

4 Add the shrimp to the sauce, blend well, then thicken the sauce with the cornstarch paste. Stir until smooth and add the sesame oil.

5 Serve hot, garnished with fresh cilantro leaves.

SWEET & SOUR SAUCE

It is now possible to buy sweet and sour sauce in bottles. They are really handy if you are short of time, but they are no match for the homemade version, which has a much subtler flavor.

STEP 2

STEP 3

STEP 4

STEP 5

FRIED SQUID FLOWERS

The addition of green bell pepper and black bean sauce to the squid makes a colorful and delicious dish from the Cantonese school.

SERVES 4

*12–14 oz prepared and cleaned squid (see
    below right)
1 medium green bell pepper, cored and
    seeded
3–4 tbsp vegetable oil
1 garlic clove, finely chopped
¼ tsp finely chopped gingerroot
2 tsp finely chopped scallions
½ tsp salt
2 tbsp crushed black bean sauce
1 tsp Chinese rice wine or dry sherry
a few drops sesame oil*

1 If ready-prepared squid is not
available, prepare as instructed in
the box, below right.

2 Open up the squid and score the
inside of the flesh in a criss-cross
pattern with a cleaver or kitchen knife.

3 Cut the squid into pieces about the
size of an oblong postage stamp.
Blanch in a bowl of boiling water for a
few seconds. Remove and drain; dry well
on paper towels.

4 Cut the bell pepper into small
triangular pieces. Heat the oil in a
preheated wok. Stir-fry the bell pepper for

about 1 minute. Add the garlic, ginger,
scallions, salt and squid. Continue stir-
frying for another minute.

5 Finally add the black bean sauce
and wine, and blend well. Serve
hot, sprinkled with sesame oil.

TO CLEAN THE SQUID

Clean the squid by first cutting off the
head. Cut off the tentacles and reserve.
Remove the small soft bone at the base of
the tentacles and the transparent
backbone, as well as the ink bag. Peel off
the thin skin, then wash and dry well.

CANTONESE STIR-FRIED SHRIMP

This colorful and delicious dish is cooked with vegetables:
vary them according to seasonal availability.

STEP 1

SERVES 4

⅔ *cup snow peas*
½ *small carrot, thinly sliced*
8 baby corn
1 cup straw mushrooms
1-1⅓ cups raw jumbo shrimp, peeled
1 tsp salt
½ *egg white, lightly beaten*
1 tsp cornstarch paste (see page 231)
about 1¼ cups vegetable oil
1 scallion, cut into short sections
4 slices gingerroot, peeled and finely chopped
½ *tsp sugar*
1 tbsp light soy sauce
1 tsp Chinese rice wine or dry sherry
a few drops sesame oil

1 Top and tail the snow peas; cut the carrot into the same size as the snow peas; halve the baby corn and straw mushrooms.

2 Mix the shrimp with a pinch of the salt, the egg white and cornstarch paste.

3 Heat a wok over high heat for 2–3 minutes, then add the oil and heat to medium-hot before adding the shrimp; stir to separate them. Remove with a slotted spoon as soon as the color changes.

4 Pour off the oil, leaving about 1 tablespoon in the wok. Add all the vegetables and stir-fry for about 1 minute. Add the shrimp and the seasonings. Blend well. Sprinkle with the sesame oil and serve hot.

STEP 2

STEP 3

STEP 4

VEGETABLE
SELECTION

When choosing alternative vegetables, remember to select contrasting colors and textures, as shown here – one green, one orange, one yellow, etc.

BAKED CRAB WITH GINGER

The crab is interchangeable with lobster. In Chinese restaurants, only live crabs and lobsters are used, but ready-cooked ones can be used at home quite successfully.

STEP 1

STEP 2

STEP 3

STEP 4

SERVES 4

1 large or 2 medium crabs, weighing about
   1¹/₂ lb in total
2 tbsp Chinese rice wine or dry sherry
1 egg, lightly beaten
1 tbsp cornstarch
3–4 tbsp vegetable oil
1 tbsp finely chopped gingerroot
3–4 scallions, cut into sections
2 tbsp light soy sauce
1 tsp sugar
about ¹/₃ cup Chinese Stock (see page 230)
   or water
¹/₂ tsp sesame oil
cilantro leaves, to garnish

1 Cut the crab in half from the underbelly. Break off the claws and crack them with the back of the cleaver or a large kitchen knife.

2 Discard the legs and crack the shell, breaking it into several pieces. Discard the feathery gills and the stomach sac. Place in a bowl with the wine, egg and cornstarch and let marinate for 10–15 minutes.

3 Heat the oil in a preheated wok and stir-fry the crab with ginger and scallions for 2–3 minutes.

4 Add the soy sauce, sugar and stock or water, blend well and bring to a boil. Cover and cook for 3–4 minutes, then remove the cover, sprinkle with sesame oil and serve.

TECHNIQUES

The term "baked" may be used on Chinese restaurant menus to describe dishes such as this one, which are actually cooked in a wok. "Pot-roasted" may be a more accurate way to describe this cooking technique.

BUYING CRABS

Crabs are almost always sold ready-cooked. The crab should feel heavy for its size, and when it is shaken, there should be no sound of water inside. A good medium-sized crab should yield about 1 lb meat, enough for 3–4 people.

FISH WITH BLACK BEAN SAUCE

Any firm and delicate fish steaks such as salmon or turbot can be cooked by the same method.

STEP 1

SERVES 4–6

1 sea bass, trout or turbot, weighing about
   1¹/₂ lb, cleaned
1 tsp salt
1 tbsp sesame oil
2–3 scallions, cut in half lengthwise
1 tbsp light soy sauce
1 tbsp Chinese rice wine or dry sherry
1 tbsp finely shredded gingerroot
1 tbsp oil
2 tbsp crushed black bean sauce
2 finely shredded scallions
cilantro leaves, to garnish (optional)
lemon slices, to garnish

1 Score both sides of the fish with diagonal cuts at 1-inch intervals. Rub both the inside and outside of the fish with salt and sesame oil.

2 Place the fish on top of the scallions on a heatproof platter. Blend the soy sauce and wine with the ginger shreds and pour evenly all over the fish.

3 Place the fish on the platter in a very hot steamer (or inside a wok on a rack), cover and steam vigorously over boiling water for 12–15 minutes or until the flesh flakes easily.

4 Heat the oil until hot, then blend in the black bean sauce. Remove the fish and place on a serving dish. Pour the hot black bean sauce over the whole length of the fish and place the shredded scallions on top. Serve garnished with cilantro leaves and lemon slices.

STEP 2

STEP 3

FISH STEAKS

If using fish steaks, rub them with the salt and sesame oil, but do not score with a knife. The fish may require less cooking, depending on the thickness of the steaks – test for doneness with a skewer after about 8 minutes.

STEP 4

STEP 1

STEP 2

STEP 3

STEP 4

CHICKEN FU-YUNG

Strictly speaking, a fu-yung dish (the name means white lotus petals) should use egg whites only to create a very delicate texture. But most people associate fu-yung with an omelet in Chinese restaurants.

SERVES 4

6 oz chicken breast fillet, skinned
1/2 tsp salt
pepper
1 tsp rice wine or dry sherry
1 tbsp cornstarch
3 eggs, beaten
1/2 tsp finely chopped scallions
3 tbsp vegetable oil
1 cup green peas
1 tsp light soy sauce
salt
few drops sesame oil

1 Cut the chicken across the grain into very small, paper-thin slices, using the cleaver. Place the slices in a shallow dish, add the half teaspoon salt, pepper, wine and cornstarch and turn in the mixture until they are well coated.

2 Beat the eggs in a small bowl with a pinch of salt and the scallions.

3 Heat oil in a preheated wok. Add chicken slices and stir-fry for about 1 minute, making sure that the slices are kept separated. Pour the beaten eggs over the chicken, and lightly scramble until set. Do not stir too vigorously, or the mixture will break up in the oil. Stir

the oil from the bottom of the wok so that the fu-yung rises to the surface.

4 Add the peas, salt and soy sauce and blend well. Sprinkle with sesame oil and serve.

VARIATION

If available, chicken *goujons* can be used for this dish: these are small, delicate strips of chicken which require no further cutting and are very tender.

LEMON CHICKEN

Lemon sauce is a Cantonese specialty, easily available in bottles from Oriental stores, or you can make your own.

STEP 1

SERVES 4

12 oz chicken breast fillets, skinned
1 tbsp rice wine or dry sherry
1 egg, beaten
4 tbsp all-purpose flour blended with 2 tbsp
   water
vegetable oil for deep-frying
ready-made lemon sauce, or homemade
   sauce (see right)
salt and pepper
fresh lemon slices, to garnish

1 Cut the chicken into thin slices and place in a shallow dish with wine, salt and pepper. Let marinate for 25–30 minutes.

2 Make a batter with the egg and flour paste. Place the chicken slices in the batter and turn to coat well.

3 Heat the oil in a preheated wok or a deep-fryer. Deep-fry the chicken slices until golden brown, remove with a slotted spoon and drain on paper towels. Cut the chicken into bite-sized pieces.

4 Heat about 1 tablespoon oil in a preheated wok. Stir in the lemon sauce until well blended and pour over the chicken. Garnish with lemon slices.

LEMON SAUCE:
1 tbsp vegetable oil
1 cup Chinese Stock (see page 230)
1 tbsp superfine sugar
1 tbsp lemon juice
1 tbsp cornstarch
1 tsp salt
1 tsp grated lemon rind

Heat the oil in a preheated wok until hot, reduce the heat and add all the other ingredients. Blend well, then bring to a boil and stir until smooth.

STEP 2

STEP 3

BOTTLED SAUCES

Many ready-made sauces are now available, and they are very useful if you are short of time. However, try to find time to make this homemade lemon sauce which has a delicious fresh taste.

STEP 4

STEP 1

STEP 2

STEP 3

STEP 4

CHICKEN WITH BEAN SPROUTS

This is the basic Chicken Chop Suey to be found in almost every Chinese restaurant and takeout throughout the world.

SERVES 4

4 oz chicken breast fillet, skinned
1 tsp salt
¹/₄ egg white, lightly beaten
2 tsp cornstarch paste (see page 231)
about 1¹/₄ cups vegetable oil
1 small onion, thinly shredded
1 small green bell pepper, cored, seeded
   and thinly shredded
1 small carrot, thinly shredded
1¹/₃ cups fresh bean sprouts
¹/₂ tsp sugar
1 tbsp light soy sauce
1 tsp rice wine or dry sherry
2–3 tbsp Chinese Stock (see page 230)
a few drops sesame oil
chili sauce, to serve

1 Thinly shred the chicken and mix with a pinch of the salt, the egg white and cornstarch paste.

2 Heat the oil in a preheated wok and stir-fry the chicken for about 1 minute, stirring to separate the shreds. Remove with a slotted spoon and drain on paper towels.

3 Pour off the oil, leaving about 2 tablespoons in the wok. Add all the vegetables except the bean sprouts.

Stir-fry for about 2 minutes, then add the bean sprouts and stir for a few seconds.

4 Return the chicken to the wok with the remaining salt, sugar, soy sauce and wine, blend well and add the stock or water. Sprinkle with the sesame oil and serve at once.

CHICKEN CHOP SUEY

Chop Suey actually originated in San Francisco at the turn of the century when Chinese immigrants were first settling there, and was first devised as a handy dish for using up leftovers.

STEP 1

STEP 2

STEP 3

STEP 4

CHICKEN WITH MUSHROOMS

*Dried Chinese mushrooms (shiitake) should be used for this dish –
otherwise use black rather than white fresh mushrooms.*

SERVES 4

10–12 oz chicken, boned and skinned
½ tsp sugar
1 tbsp light soy sauce
1 tsp rice wine or dry sherry
2 tsp cornstarch
4–6 dried Chinese mushrooms, soaked in
*   warm water*
1 tbsp finely shredded gingerroot
salt and pepper
a few drops sesame oil
cilantro leaves, to garnish

1 Cut the chicken into small bite-sized pieces and place in a bowl. Add the sugar, soy sauce, wine and cornstarch and let marinate for 25–30 minutes.

2 Drain the mushrooms and dry on paper towels. Slice the mushrooms into thin shreds, discarding any hard pieces of stem.

3 Place the chicken pieces on a heatproof dish that will fit inside a bamboo steamer. Arrange the mushroom and ginger shreds on top of the chicken and sprinkle with salt, pepper and sesame oil.

4 Place the dish on the rack inside a hot steamer or on a rack in a wok filled with hot water. Steam over high heat for 20 minutes. Serve hot, garnished with cilantro leaves.

CHINESE MUSHROOMS

Chinese mushrooms come in many varieties: Shiitake are the best, and the two terms are often used synonymously. These fragrant mushrooms are most readily available at Oriental food stores and supermarkets but are also seasonally available.

Do not throw away the soaking water from the dried Chinese mushrooms. It is very useful, as it can be added to soups and stocks to give extra flavor.

STEP 1

STEP 2

STEP 3

STEP 4

DUCK WITH PINEAPPLE

For best results, use ready-cooked duck meat, widely available from Chinese restaurants and takeouts.

SERVES 4

about 1 cup cooked duck meat
3 tbsp vegetable oil
1 small onion, thinly shredded
2–3 slices gingerroot, thinly shredded
1 scallion, thinly shredded
1 small carrot, thinly shredded
²/₃ cup canned pineapple, cut into small slices
¹/₂ tsp salt
1 tbsp red rice vinegar
2 tbsp syrup from the pineapple
1 tbsp cornstarch paste (see page 231)
black bean sauce, to serve (optional)

1 Cut the cooked duck meat into thin strips.

2 Heat the oil in a preheated wok. Add the shredded onion and stir-fry until the shreds are opaque. Add the ginger, scallion and carrot shreds. Stir-fry for about 1 minute.

3 Add the duck shreds and pineapple to the wok together with the salt, rice vinegar and the pineapple syrup. Stir until the mixture is blended well.

4 Add the cornstarch paste and stir for 1–2 minutes until the sauce has thickened. Serve hot.

CANNED PINEAPPLE

Fortunately, most canned fruit is now available preserved in juice rather than syrup. The sugared syrup once used exclusively for this purpose was cloyingly sweet. To prepare this dish, be sure to choose pineapple in juice rather than syrup, so that the sauce is pleasantly tangy rather than overwhelmingly sugary.

STEP 1

STEP 2

STEP 3

STEP 4

STIR-FRIED PORK WITH VEGETABLES

*This is a basic "meat and vegetables" recipe – the meat can be pork,
chicken, beef or lamb, and the vegetables can be varied according to
seasonal availability.*

SERVES 4

8 oz pork tenderloin, sliced
1 tsp sugar
1 tbsp light soy sauce
1 tsp rice wine or dry sherry
1 tsp cornstarch paste (see page 231)
1 small carrot
1 small green bell pepper, cored and seeded
about 1½–2 cups Chinese leaves
4 tbsp vegetable oil
1 scallion, cut into short sections
a few small peeled gingerroot slices
1 tsp salt
2–3 tbsp Chinese Stock (see page 230) or
    water
a few drops sesame oil

1 Thinly slice the pork tenderloin
into small pieces and place in a
shallow dish. Add half the sugar and the
soy sauce, the wine and cornstarch paste.
Place in the refrigerator and marinate for
10–15 minutes.

2 Cut the carrot, green bell pepper
and Chinese leaves into thin slices
roughly the same length and width as
the pork pieces so they cook in the same
amount of time.

3 Heat the oil in a preheated wok.
Stir-fry the pork for about 1 minute
to seal in the flavor. Remove with a
slotted spoon and keep warm.

4 Add the carrot, bell pepper, Chinese
leaves, scallion and ginger and stir-
fry for about 2 minutes.

5 Add the salt and remaining sugar,
followed by the pork and remaining
soy sauce, and the stock or water. Blend
well and stir for another 1–2 minutes
until hot. Sprinkle with the sesame oil
and serve.

VARIATIONS

This dish can be made with other meats,
as mentioned in the introduction. If using
chicken strips, reduce the initial cooking
time in the wok.

STEP 1

STEP 2

STEP 3

STEP 4

SWEET & SOUR PORK

*This has to be the most popular Chinese dish all over the world.
The pork can be replaced with almost any other ingredient:
fish, shrimp, chicken or even vegetables.*

SERVES 4

8–10 oz lean pork
2 tsp brandy or whisky
vegetable oil, for deep-frying
1 egg, beaten
2 tbsp all-purpose flour
salt and pepper

SAUCE:
1 tbsp vegetable oil
1 small onion, diced
1 small carrot, diced
¹/₂ small green bell pepper, cored, seeded
*   and diced*
1 tbsp light soy sauce
3 tbsp sugar
3 tbsp wine vinegar
1 tbsp tomato paste
about 3–4 tbsp Chinese Stock (see page
*   230) or water*
1 tbsp cornstarch paste (see page 231)

1 Cut the pork into small bite-sized
cubes. Place in a dish with the salt,
pepper and brandy and let marinate for
15–20 minutes.

2 Heat the oil in a preheated wok or a
deep-fryer. Place the pork cubes in
a bowl with the beaten egg and stir to
ensure an all-over covering. Sprinkle on

the flour and turn the pork cubes until
they are well coated.

3 Deep-fry the pork cubes in batches
for 3–4 minutes, stirring gently to
separate the pieces. Remove with a
slotted spoon or strainer and drain on
paper towels. Reheat the oil until hot,
and return the meat to the wok for
another minute or so or until golden
brown. Remove with a slotted spoon and
drain on paper towels.

4 To make the sauce, heat the oil in a
preheated wok or pan. Add the
vegetables and stir-fry for about 1
minute. Add the seasonings and tomato
paste with stock or water, bring to a boil
and thicken with the cornstarch paste.

5 Add the pork and blend well so that
each piece of meat is coated with
the sauce. Serve hot.

SPARERIBS WITH CHILI

For best results, chop the spareribs into small bite-size pieces.

STEP 1

SERVES 4

1 lb pork spareribs
1 tsp sugar
1 tbsp light soy sauce
1 tsp rice wine or dry sherry
1 tsp cornstarch
about 2 ¹/₂ cups vegetable oil
1 garlic clove, finely chopped
1 scallion, cut into short sections
1 small hot chili pepper (green or red),
    thinly sliced
2 tbsp black bean sauce
about ²/₃ cup Chinese Stock (see page 230)
    or water
1 small onion, diced
1 green bell pepper, cored, seeded and diced

1 Trim excess fat from the ribs, and chop each one into 3–4 bite-sized pieces. Place the ribs in a shallow dish with the sugar, soy sauce, wine and cornstarch and let marinate for 35–45 minutes.

2 Heat the oil in a preheated wok. Add the spareribs and deep-fry for 2–3 minutes until light brown. Remove with a slotted spoon and drain well on paper towels.

3 Pour off the oil, leaving about 1 tablespoon in the wok. Add the garlic, scallion, chili pepper and black bean sauce and stir-fry for 30–40 seconds.

4 Add the spareribs, blend well, then add the stock or water. Bring to a boil, then reduce the heat, cover and braise for 8–10 minutes, stirring once or twice.

5 Add the onion and green bell pepper, increase the heat to high, and stir uncovered for about 2 minutes to reduce the sauce a little. Serve hot.

STEP 2

STEP 3

HANDLING CHILIES

Be very careful when handling and cutting chili peppers as they exude a juice which can cause irritation of the skin. Be sure to wash your hands after handling, and keep well away from face and eyes. It is the seeds of the chili that are the hottest part – remove seeds if you do not want a very hot dish.

STEP 5

STEP 1

STEP 2

STEP 3

STEP 4

OYSTER SAUCE BEEF

*Like Stir-fried Pork with Vegetables (see page 54), the vegetables used in
this recipe can be varied as you wish.*

SERVES 4

10 oz beef steak
1 tsp sugar
1 tbsp light soy sauce
1 tsp rice wine or dry sherry
1 tsp cornstarch paste (see page 231)
$^{1}/_{2}$ small carrot
$^{2}/_{3}$ cup snow peas
$^{1}/_{3}$ cup canned bamboo shoots, rinsed and
    drained
1 cup canned straw mushrooms, rinsed and
    drained
about 1$^{1}/_{4}$ cups vegetable oil
1 scallion, cut into short sections
2–3 small slices gingerroot
$^{1}/_{2}$ tsp salt
2 tbsp oyster sauce
2–3 tbsp Chinese Stock (see page 230)
    or water

1 Cut the beef into small, thin slices.
Place in a shallow dish with the
sugar, soy sauce, wine and cornstarch
paste and let marinate for 25–30
minutes.

2 Slice the carrots, snow peas,
bamboo shoots and straw
mushrooms so that as far as possible the
vegetable pieces are of uniform size and
thickness so they cook in the same time.

3 Heat the oil in a preheated wok.
Add the beef slices and stir-fry for
about 1 minute, then remove with a
slotted spoon and keep warm.

4 Pour off the oil, leaving about 1
tablespoon in the wok. Add the
sliced vegetables with the scallion and
ginger and stir-fry for about 2 minutes.
Add the salt, beef and the oyster sauce
with stock or water. Blend well until
heated through, and serve with a dip
sauce, if liked.

VARIATIONS

You can use whatever vegetables are
available for this dish, but it is important
to get a good contrast of color – don't use
all red or all green for example.

CHAPTER FOUR

Vegetables

Being basically an agricultural country, China has really perfected vegetable cooking into a fine art – almost all are cooked for a very short time, thus preserving their natural flavors and textures, as well as the vitamins and the brightness of their colors.

The Chinese eat far more vegetables than meat or poultry, and with a few exceptions, almost all meat and poultry dishes include some kind of vegetable as a supplementary ingredient – the idea being to give the dish a harmonious balance of color, aroma, flavor and texture.

When selecting vegetables for cooking, the Chinese attach great importance to the freshness of ingredients used. Always buy crisp, firm vegetables, and cook them as soon as possible. Another point to remember is to wash the vegetables just before cutting, in order to avoid losing vitamins in water, and to cook them as soon as they have been cut so that the vitamin content is not lost through evaporation.

Opposite: *A stallholder in Mongolia proudly displays his selection of fruits and vegetables. Chinese cooks attach great importance to freshness, and visit the market daily to buy fresh produce for the family meal.*

STEP 1

STEP 2

STEP 3

STEP 4

STIR-FRIED MIXED VEGETABLES

The Chinese never mix ingredients indiscriminately – they are carefully selected to achieve a harmonious balance of contrasting colors and textures.

SERVES 4

²/₃ cup snow peas
1 small carrot
1¹/₄ cups Chinese leaves
2 cups fresh bean sprouts
1 cup black or white mushrooms
²/₃ cup canned bamboo shoots, rinsed
   and drained
3–4 tbsp vegetable oil
1 tsp salt
1 tsp sugar
1 tbsp oyster sauce or light soy sauce
a few drops sesame oil (optional)
dipping sauce, to serve (optional)

1 Prepare the vegetables: top and tail the snow peas, and cut the carrot, Chinese leaves, mushrooms and bamboo shoots into roughly the same shape and size as the snow peas.

2 Heat the oil in a preheated wok, and add the carrot first. Stir-fry for a few seconds, then add the snow peas and Chinese leaves and stir-fry for about 1 minute.

3 Add the bean sprouts, mushrooms and bamboo shoots and stir-fry for another minute.

4 Add the salt and sugar, continue stirring for another minute, then add the oyster sauce or soy sauce, blend well, and sprinkle with sesame oil (if using). Serve hot or cold, with a dip sauce, if liked.

OYSTER SAUCE

This sauce, made from oysters cooked with salt and spices, is used in many Cantonese dishes. It is worth spending a little more on a good bottle of oyster sauce, as the more expensive brands are noticeably better. Good oyster sauce has a rich, almost beefy flavor. Once opened, a bottle of oyster sauce can be kept for months in the refrigerator and used to flavor a range of Oriental dishes.

BEAN-SPROUTS

It is important to use fresh bean-sprouts for this dish – the canned ones don't have the crunchy texture that is vital. If fresh ones are unavailable, select another vegetable, remembering to keep a color contrast.

STEP 1

STEP 2

STEP 3

STEP 4

BROCCOLI IN OYSTER SAUCE

Some Cantonese restaurants use only the stems of the broccoli for this dish, for the crunchy texture.

SERVES 4

8–10 oz broccoli
3 tbsp vegetable oil
3–4 small slices gingerroot
$\frac{1}{2}$ tsp salt
$\frac{1}{2}$ tsp sugar
3–4 tbsp Chinese Stock (see page 230) or
   water
1 tbsp oyster sauce

1 Cut the broccoli spears into small flowerets. Trim the stems, peel off the rough skin, and cut the stems diagonally into diamond-shaped chunks.

2 Heat the oil in a preheated wok and add the pieces of broccoli stem and the ginger. Stir-fry for about 30 seconds, then add the broccoli flowerets. Continue to stir-fry for another 2 minutes.

3 Add the salt, sugar and stock or water, and continue stirring for another minute or so.

4 Blend in the oyster sauce. Serve hot or leave until cold.

BROCCOLI STEMS

The broccoli stems have to be peeled and cut diagonally to ensure they cook evenly. If they are thin, the pieces can be added to the wok at the same time as the florets, but otherwise add the stems first, to ensure they will be tender.

VARIATION

Any crunchy-textured vegetable can be used in this recipe. If preferred, you could use cauliflower, celery, zucchini, green beans, etc., making sure that they are cut into even-sized pieces.

BRAISED CHINESE VEGETABLES

This dish is also known as Lo Han Zhai or Buddha's Delight. The original recipe calls for no less than 18 different vegetables to represent the 18 Buddhas (Lo Han) but six to eight are quite acceptable.

STEP 1

STEP 2

STEP 3

STEP 5

SERVES 4

¹/₄ cup dried wood ears
1 cake tofu
²/₃ cup snow peas
1¹/₄ cups Chinese leaves
1 small carrot
about 12 canned baby corn, drained
1¹/₂ cups canned straw mushrooms, rinsed
    and drained
¹/₃ cup canned water chestnuts, rinsed and
    drained
1¹/₄ cups vegetable oil
1 tsp salt
¹/₂ tsp sugar
1 tbsp light soy sauce or oyster sauce
2–3 tbsp Chinese Stock (see page 230) or
    water
a few drops sesame oil

1 Soak the wood ears in warm water for 15–20 minutes, then rinse and drain, discarding any hard bits. Dry on paper towels.

2 Cut the cake of tofu into about 18 small pieces. Top and tail the snow peas. Cut the Chinese leaves and the carrot into slices roughly the same size and shape as the snow peas. Cut the baby corn, the straw mushrooms and the water chestnuts in half.

3 Heat the oil in a preheated wok. Add the tofu and deep-fry for about 2 minutes until it turns slightly golden. Remove with a slotted spoon and drain on paper towels.

4 Pour off the oil, leaving about 2 tablespoons in the wok. Add the carrot, Chinese leaves and snow peas and stir-fry for about 1 minute.

5 Add the baby corn, mushrooms and water chestnuts. Stir gently for 2 more minutes, then add the salt, sugar, soy sauce and stock or water. Bring to a boil and stir-fry for 1 more minute.

6 Sprinkle with sesame oil and serve hot or cold.

WOOD EARS

Wood ears (a kind of fungus) can usually be obtained in Chinese supermarkets. If unavailable, use another variety of Chinese mushrooms.

STEP 1

STEP 2

STEP 3

STEP 4

STIR-FRIED BEAN SPROUTS

Be sure to use fresh bean-sprouts, rather than the canned variety, for this crunchy-textured dish.

SERVES 4

4 cups fresh bean sprouts
2–3 scallions
1 red chili pepper (optional)
3 tbsp vegetable oil
1/2 tsp salt
1/2 tsp sugar
1 tbsp light soy sauce
a few drops sesame oil (optional)

1 Rinse the bean sprouts in cold water, discarding any husks or small pieces that float to the top. Drain well on paper towels.

2 Cut the scallions into short sections. Thinly shred the red chili pepper, if using, discarding the seeds.

3 Heat the oil in a preheated wok. Add the bean sprouts, scallions and chili pepper, if using, and stir-fry for about 2 minutes.

4 Add the salt, sugar, soy sauce and sesame oil, if using, to the mixture in the wok. Stir well to blend. Serve hot or cold.

TO GROW BEAN SPROUTS

It is very easy to grow bean sprouts. If you find it difficult to buy fresh ones, this could be the answer. Use dried mung beans, obtainable from supermarkets and health-food stores. Wash the beans thoroughly in several changes of water. Place in a lidded jar, or a seed sprouter if you have one, and place in a warm, dark place (an airing closet is ideal). Check daily and rinse with a little water to keep them moist. You should have sprouts that are ready to use in 3–4 days.

VARIATION

The red chili pepper gives a bite to this dish – leave the seeds in for an even hotter taste. If you prefer a milder, sweeter flavor, use red bell pepper instead of the chili pepper. Core, seed and cut into strips in the same way.

CHAPTER FIVE

Rice & Noodles

Rice and noodles provide bulk in the Chinese diet, but the recipes given here are meant to be served on their own, as a light meal or as a snack. For an everyday meal, plain rice is served with two or three other dishes – usually meat and vegetables together with a soup. Fried rice and chow mein are only served at formal occasions, or as a snack between main meals.

In China, noodles are always served at birthday celebrations, as the Chinese consider that the length of noodles symbolizes long life.

The Chinese do not normally conclude an everyday meal with a dessert, but fresh fruit can always be served for those who are used to finishing off a meal with something sweet.

Opposite: *A woman tends the irrigation system in rice paddy fields near Guilin. Rice is the most important staple in the Chinese diet, and vast tracts of fertile land are given over to its cultivation.*

STEP 1

STEP 3

STEP 3

STEP 5

SEAFOOD CHOW MEIN

*Use whatever seafood is available for this delicious noodle dish –
mussels or crab would also be suitable. Simply add to the wok with
the other seafood in step 6.*

SERVES 4

3 oz squid, cleaned (see page 36)
3–4 fresh scallops
$\frac{1}{2}$ cup raw shrimp, peeled
$\frac{1}{2}$ egg white, lightly beaten
1 tbsp cornstarch paste (see page 231)
$\frac{1}{2}$ lb Chinese egg noodles
5–6 tbsp vegetable oil
2 tbsp light soy sauce
$\frac{2}{3}$ cup snow peas
$\frac{1}{2}$ tsp salt
$\frac{1}{2}$ tsp sugar
1 tsp Chinese rice wine or dry sherry
2 scallions, finely shredded
a few drops sesame oil

1 Open up the squid and score the
inside in a criss-cross pattern, then
cut into pieces, each about the size of a
postage stamp.

2 Soak the squid in a bowl of boiling
water until all the pieces curl up.
Rinse in cold water and drain.

3 Cut each scallop into 3–4 slices.
Cut the shrimp in half lengthwise if
large. Mix the scallops and shrimp with
the egg white and cornstarch paste.

4 Cook the noodles in boiling water
according to the instructions on
the package, then drain and rinse under
cold water. Drain well, then toss with
about 1 tablespoon of oil.

5 Heat 3 tablespoons oil in a
preheated wok. Add the noodles
and 1 tablespoon of the soy sauce and
stir-fry for 2–3 minutes. Remove to a
large serving dish.

6 Heat the remaining oil in the wok
and add the snow peas and seafood.
Stir-fry for about 2 minutes, then add the
salt, sugar, wine, remaining soy sauce
and about half the scallions. Blend well
and add a little stock or water if
necessary.

7 Pour the seafood mixture on top of
the noodles and sprinkle with
sesame oil. Garnish with the remaining
scallions and serve hot or at room
temperature.

FRIED NOODLES (CHOW MEIN)

This is a basic recipe for Chow Mein. Additional ingredients such as vegetables (see page 144), chicken or pork (see page 220), or seafood (see page 74) can be added if liked.

STEP 1

SERVES 4

½ lb Chinese egg noodles
3–4 tbsp vegetable oil
1 small onion, finely shredded
2 cups fresh bean sprouts
1 scallion, finely shredded
2 tbsp light soy sauce
a few drops sesame oil

1 Cook the noodles in salted boiling water according to the instructions on the package (usually no more than 4–5 minutes).

2 Drain and rinse the noodles in cold water; drain well, then toss with a little vegetable oil.

3 Heat the remaining oil in a preheated wok. Stir-fry the onion for about 30–40 seconds, then add the bean sprouts and noodles, stir and toss for 1 more minute.

4 Add the scallion and soy sauce and blend well. Sprinkle with the sesame oil and serve.

STEP 2

FRESH NOODLES

Chinese egg noodles are made from wheat or rice flour, water and egg. Handmade noodles are made by an elaborate process of kneading, pulling and twisting the dough, and it takes years to learn the art. Noodles are a symbol of longevity, and so are always served at birthday celebrations – it is regarded as bad luck to cut them. If fresh egg noodles are available, these require very little cooking: simply place in boiling water for about 3 minutes, then drain and toss in oil. Noodles can be boiled and eaten plain, or stir-fried with meat and vegetables for a light meal or snack.

STEP 3

STEP 4

STEP 1

STEP 2

STEP 3

STEP 4

SINGAPORE-STYLE RICE NOODLES

Rice noodles or vermicelli are also known as rice sticks. Egg noodles can also be used for this dish, but it will not taste the same. The ideal meat to use is Barbecue Pork (see page 22).

SERVES 4

1/2 lb rice vermicelli
1 cup cooked chicken or pork
1/2 cup peeled shrimp, defrosted if frozen
4 tbsp vegetable oil
1 onion, thinly shredded
2 cups fresh bean sprouts
1 tsp salt
1 tbsp mild curry powder
2 tbsp light soy sauce
2 scallions, thinly shredded
1–2 small fresh green or red chili peppers,
   seeded and thinly shredded

1 Soak the rice vermicelli in boiling water for 8–10 minutes, then rinse in cold water and drain well.

2 Thinly slice the cooked meat. Dry the shrimp thoroughly on paper towels.

3 Heat the oil in a preheated wok. Add the onion and stir-fry until opaque. Add the bean sprouts and stir-fry for 1 minute.

4 Add the noodles with the meat and shrimp, and continue stirring for another minute.

5 Blend in the salt, curry powder and soy sauce, followed by the scallions and chili peppers. Stir-fry for 1 more minute, then serve at once.

RICE NOODLES

Rice noodles are very delicate noodles made from rice flour. They become soft and pliable after being soaked for about 15 minutes. If you wish to store them after they have been soaked, toss them in a few drops of sesame oil, then place them in a sealed container in the refrigerator.

VARIATION

For a really authentic flavor include 1 tablespoon dried shrimps, which have a strong, pungent taste. Soak them in warm water for 30 minutes, drain and add to the noodles in step 4.

STEP 1

STEP 2

STEP 3

STEP 4

SPECIAL FRIED RICE

Special Fried Rice, sometimes called Yangchow Fried Rice, is almost a meal in itself. Make sure the cooked rice is completely dry and cold before adding it to the wok, otherwise it might stick and become lumpy.

SERVES 4

½ cup peeled shrimp
½ cup cooked meat (chicken, pork or ham)
1 cup green peas
3 eggs
1 tsp salt
2 scallions, finely chopped
4 tbsp vegetable oil
1 tbsp light soy sauce
1 tsp Chinese rice wine or dry sherry
  (optional)
4 cups cooked rice

1 Dry the shrimp on paper towels. Cut the meat into small dice about the same size as the peas.

2 In a bowl, lightly beat the eggs with a pinch of salt and a few pieces of the scallions.

3 Heat 2 tablespoons of the oil in a preheated wok. Add the peas, shrimp and meat and stir-fry for about 1 minute. Stir in the soy sauce and wine, then remove and keep warm.

4 Heat the remaining oil and add the eggs. Stir to lightly scramble. Add the rice and stir to separate the grains, then add the remaining salt and

scallions, and the shrimp, meat and peas. Blend well and serve hot or cold.

FRESH PEAS

Fresh peas straight from the shell really do make a difference to this dish. Their vivid, emerald color and just-off-the-vine flavor make it worth the (relatively small) amount of effort. Shell and lightly blanch the peas before stir-frying them.

PERFECT RICE

Cook the rice by the absorption method as described on page 232. Let stand, covered, until the rice has absorbed all the water, then turn out on to a large flat plate or cookie sheet. Spread the rice out and leave until completely cold and dry.

CHAPTER SIX

Appetizers

A selection of small portions of several different dishes usually starts the Chinese meal. The majority of these appetizers consist of tasty fillings enclosed in pastry-type wrappers which are fried until crisp. These are served with a simple dipping sauce of soy sauce, sherry and strips of scallion and chili.

Snacks and appetizers are also sold at many roadside stalls throughout China, and are bought and eaten by people as they go about their daily tasks. After dusk, the sidewalks are filled with groups of families and friends cooking, eating and selling many delicious meals; this is an important part of their social lives, and is an enjoyable way of getting together and sharing their food.

Use the dishes in this section as appetizers to the main meal, or as snacks in their own right.

Opposite: *Hong Kong harbor shrouded in mist.*

STEP 1

STEP 2

STEP 3

STEP 4

CRISPY WONTONS WITH PIQUANT DIPPING SAUCE

Mushroom-filled crispy wontons are served on skewers with a dipping sauce flavored with chilies.

SERVES 4

1 tbsp vegetable oil
1 tbsp chopped onion
1 small garlic clove, chopped
1/2 tsp chopped gingerroot
1/2 cup flat mushrooms, chopped
16 wonton skins (see page 100)
vegetable oil for deep-frying
salt
8 wooden skewers

SAUCE:
2 tbsp vegetable oil
2 scallions, thinly shredded
1 red and 1 green chili, seeded and thinly
    shredded
3 tbsp light soy sauce
1 tbsp vinegar
1 tbsp dry sherry
pinch sugar

1 Heat the oil in a preheated wok or skillet. Add the onion, garlic and gingerroot, and stir-fry for 2 minutes. Stir in the mushrooms and fry for a further 2 minutes. Season well with salt and let cool.

2 Place 1 teaspoon of the cooled mushroom filling in the center of each wonton skin. Bring 2 opposite corners together to cover the mixture and pinch together to seal. Repeat with the remaining corners.

3 Thread 2 wontons on to each skewer. Heat enough oil in a large saucepan to deep-fry the wontons in batches until golden and crisp. Remove with a perforated spoon and drain on paper towels.

4 To make the sauce, heat the oil in a small saucepan until quite hot and a small cube of bread dropped in the oil browns in a few seconds. Put the scallions and chilies in a bowl and pour the hot oil slowly on top. Then mix in the remaining ingredients and serve with the crispy wontons.

HEATING THE OIL

Do not overheat the oil for deep-frying, or the wontons will brown on the outside before they are properly cooked inside.

STEP 2

STEP 3

STEP 4

STEP 5

CRISPY SEAWEED

Popular in many Chinese restaurants, this dish is served as a first course. This "seaweed" is, in fact, deep-fried spring greens.

SERVES 4

8 oz spring greens
vegetable oil for deep-frying
1 1/2 tsp superfine sugar
1 tsp salt
1/4 cup slivered almonds

1 Wash the spring greens thoroughly. Trim off the excess tough stems. Place on paper towels or a dry dish cloth and let drain thoroughly.

2 Using a sharp knife, shred the spring greens finely and spread out on several layers of paper towels for about 30 minutes to dry.

3 Heat the oil in a preheated wok or deep-fryer. Remove the pan from the heat and add the spring greens in batches. Return the pan to the heat and deep-fry until the greens begin to float to the surface and become translucent and crinkled. Remove the spring greens, using a perforated spoon, and drain on paper towels. Keep each batch warm.

4 Mix the sugar and salt together, sprinkle over the "seaweed" and toss together to mix well.

5 Add the slivered almonds to the hot oil and fry until lightly golden. Remove with a perforated spoon and drain on paper towels.

6 Serve the crispy "seaweed" with the slivered almonds.

TIME-SAVER

As a time-saver you can use a food processor to shred the greens finely. Make sure you use only the best of the leaves; sort through the spring greens and discard any tough outer leaves, as these will spoil the overall taste and texture if they are included.

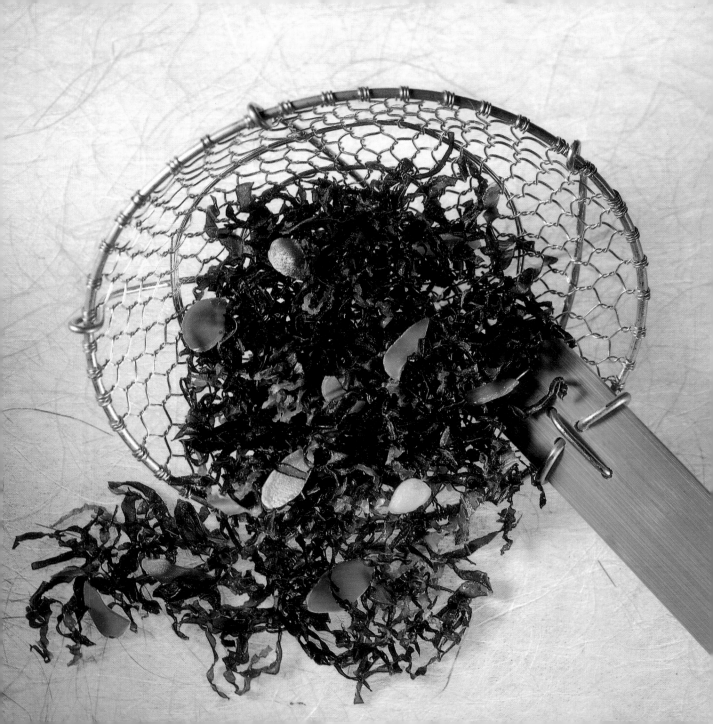

TOFU SANDWICHES

Slices of tofu are sandwiched together with a cucumber and cream cheese filling and coated in batter. Serve with a mint and yogurt dipping sauce.

STEP 2

STEP 3

MAKES 28

4 Chinese dried mushrooms (if unavailable,
   use thinly sliced open-cup mushrooms)
9 oz tofu
1/2 English cucumber, grated
1/2-inch piece gingerroot, grated
1/4 cup cream cheese
salt and pepper

BATTER:
1 cup all-purpose flour
1 egg, beaten
1/2 cup water
1/2 tsp salt
2 tbsp sesame seeds
vegetable oil for deep-frying

SAUCE:
2/3 cup natural yogurt
2 tsp honey
2 tbsp chopped fresh mint

1 Place the mushrooms in a small bowl and cover with warm water. Let soak for 20–25 minutes. Drain and squeeze out the excess water. Remove the tough centers and chop the mushrooms.

2 Drain the tofu, slice thinly and cut each slice to make 1-inch squares.

3 Squeeze the excess liquid from the cucumber and mix the cucumber with the mushrooms, grated ginger and cream cheese. Season well. Use as a filling to sandwich slices of tofu together to make about 28 sandwiches.

4 To make the batter, sift the flour into a bowl. Beat in the egg, water and salt to make a thick batter. Stir in the sesame seeds. Heat the oil in a large preheated wok or saucepan. Coat the sandwiches in the batter and deep-fry in batches until golden. Remove with a slotted spoon and drain on paper towels.

5 To make the dipping sauce, blend together the yogurt, honey and mint. Serve with the tofu sandwiches.

VARIATION

For a change you could try using smoked tofu, which will add extra flavor to the sandwiches.

STEP 4

STEP 5

STEP 2

STEP 3

STEP 4

STEP 5

EGG ROLLS

Thin slices of vegetables are wrapped in pastry and deep-fried until crisp. Egg roll wrappers are available fresh or frozen from Oriental suppliers and some supermarkets.

MAKES 12

5 Chinese dried mushrooms (if unavailable, use open-cup mushrooms)
1 large carrot
1 cup canned bamboo shoots, rinsed and drained
2 scallions
¼ head Chinese leaves
2 tbsp vegetable oil
250 g/8 oz/4 cups bean sprouts
1 tbsp soy sauce
12 egg roll wrappers
1 egg, beaten
vegetable oil for deep-frying
salt

1 Place the mushrooms in a small bowl and cover with warm water. Let soak for 20–25 minutes.

2 Drain the mushrooms and squeeze out the excess water. Remove the tough centers and slice the mushrooms thinly. Cut the carrot and bamboo shoots into very thin julienne strips. Chop the scallions and shred the Chinese leaves.

3 Heat the 2 tablespoons of oil in a preheated wok or skillet. Add the mushrooms, carrot and bamboo shoots, continue stir-frying for about 2 minutes.

Add the scallions, Chinese leaves, bean sprouts and soy sauce. Season with salt and stir-fry for 2 minutes. Let cool.

4 Divide the mixture into 12 equal portions and place one portion on the edge of each egg roll wrapper. Fold in the sides and roll each one up, brushing the join with a little beaten egg to seal.

5 Deep-fry the egg rolls in batches in hot oil in a wok or large saucepan for 4–5 minutes, or until golden and crispy. Take care that the oil is not too hot or the egg rolls will brown on the outside before cooking on the inside. Remove and drain on paper towels. Keep each batch warm while the others are being cooked. Serve at once.

EGG ROLL WRAPPERS

If egg roll wrappers are unavailable, use sheets of filo pastry instead.

STEP 1

STEP 2

STEP 3

STEP 4

SWEET & SOUR CUCUMBER

Chunks of cucumber are marinated in vinegar and sweetened with honey to make a sweet and sour appetizer.

SERVES 4

1 English cucumber
1 tsp salt
2 tsp honey
2 tbsp rice vinegar
3 tbsp chopped fresh cilantro
2 tsp sesame oil
$^1/_4$ tsp crushed red peppercorns
strips of red and yellow bell pepper, to
    garnish

1 Peel thin strips off the cucumber along the length. This gives a pretty striped effect. Cut the cucumber in quarters lengthwise and then into 1-inch long pieces. Place in a colander.

2 Sprinkle the salt over the cucumber and let rest for 30 minutes to allow the salt to draw out the excess water from the cucumber. Wash the cucumber thoroughly to remove the salt, drain and pat dry with paper towels.

3 Place the cucumber in a bowl. Combine the honey with the vinegar and pour over. Mix together and let marinate for 15 minutes.

4 Stir in the cilantro and sesame oil, and place in a serving bowl.

5 Sprinkle over the crushed red peppercorns. Serve garnished with strips of red and yellow bell peppers.

RICE VINEGAR

Rice vinegar is a common Chinese cooking ingredient. White rice vinegar is made from rice wine, whereas red rice vinegar is made from fermented rice. Both have a distinctive flavor, but the white version tends to be used more often, as it will flavor but not color all kinds of food. If rice vinegar is unavailable, use white wine vinegar instead.

CHAPTER SEVEN

Soups

In China soups are not usually served at the beginning of a meal but between courses to clear the palate. It is also quite common for Chinese families to have a large tureen of clear soup on the table which is served at the same time as the other dishes. Chinese cooks will often add some boiling clear stock or water to leftovers from the main course and serve it as an instant soup at the end of the meal.

Generally the soups are made from a good stock of vegetables, which are boiled for about 30 minutes before being strained, which gives a thin, clear broth. This can be served on its own, with a little soy sauce added for flavor. With the addition of a few suitable vegetables you can make a simple but tasty soup.

Most Chinese soups are of the thin, clear variety; however they do have a few thickened ones, such as the Hot & Sour Soup to which cornstarch is added. These soups can be eaten as a lunch or snack on their own.

Opposite: *The familiar sight of a one-man "taxi" in the back streets of Hong Kong.*

STEP 1

STEP 2

STEP 3

STEP 4

VEGETARIAN HOT & SOUR SOUP

This is a popular Chinese soup, which is unusual in that it is thickened. The characteristic "hot" flavor is achieved by the addition of plenty of black pepper.

SERVES 4

4 Chinese dried mushrooms (if unavailable, use open-cup mushrooms)
4 oz firm tofu
1 cup canned bamboo shoots, rinsed and drained
2¹/₂ cups vegetable stock or water
¹/₃ cup shelled peas
1 tbsp dark soy sauce
2 tbsp white wine vinegar
2 tbsp cornstarch
salt and pepper
sesame oil, to serve

1 Place the Chinese dried mushrooms in a small bowl and cover with warm water. Let soak for 20–25 minutes.

2 Drain the mushrooms and squeeze out the excess water, reserving it. Remove the tough centers and cut the mushrooms into thin shreds. Shred the tofu and bamboo shoots.

3 Bring the stock or water to a boil in a large saucepan. Add the mushrooms, tofu, bamboo shoots and peas. Simmer for 2 minutes.

4 Mix together the soy sauce, vinegar and cornstarch with 2 tablespoons of the reserved mushroom liquid. Stir into the soup with the remaining mushroom liquid. Bring to a boil and season with salt and plenty of pepper. Simmer for 2 minutes.

5 Serve in warmed bowls with a few drops of sesame oil in each.

MUSHROOMS

If you use open-cup mushrooms instead of dried mushrooms, add an extra ²/₃ cup vegetable stock or water to the soup, as these mushrooms do not need soaking.

STEP 1

STEP 2

STEP 3

STEP 4

WONTON SOUP

Spinach and pine nut filled wontons are served in a clear soup. The recipe for the wonton skins makes 24 but the soup requires only half this quantity. The other half can be frozen ready for another time.

SERVES 4

WONTON SKINS:
1 egg
6 tbsp water
2 cups all-purpose flour

FILLING:
$^1/_2$ cup frozen chopped spinach, defrosted
1 tbsp pine nuts, toasted and chopped
$^1/_4$ cup ground TVP (soy granules)
salt

SOUP:
$2^1/_2$ cups vegetable stock
1 tbsp dry sherry
1 tbsp light soy sauce
2 scallions, chopped

1 Beat the egg lightly in a bowl and mix with the water. Stir in the flour to form a stiff dough. Knead lightly, then cover with a damp cloth and let rest for 30 minutes.

2 Roll out the dough into a large sheet about $^1/_4$-inch thick. Cut out twenty-four 3-inch squares. Dust each one lightly with flour. Only 12 squares are required for the soup so freeze the remainder (see below).

3 To make the filling, squeeze out the excess water from the spinach. Mix the spinach with the pine nuts and TVP (soy granules). Season with salt.

4 Divide the mixture into 12 equal portions and place one portion in the center of each wonton square. Seal by bringing the opposite corners of each square together and squeezing well.

5 To make the soup, bring the stock, sherry and soy sauce to a boil. Add the wontons and boil rapidly for 2–3 minutes. Add the scallions and serve in warmed bowls immediately.

FREEZING WONTON SKINS

To freeze the leftover wonton skins, place small squares of baking parchment in between each skin, then place in a freezer bag and freeze. Defrost thoroughly before using.

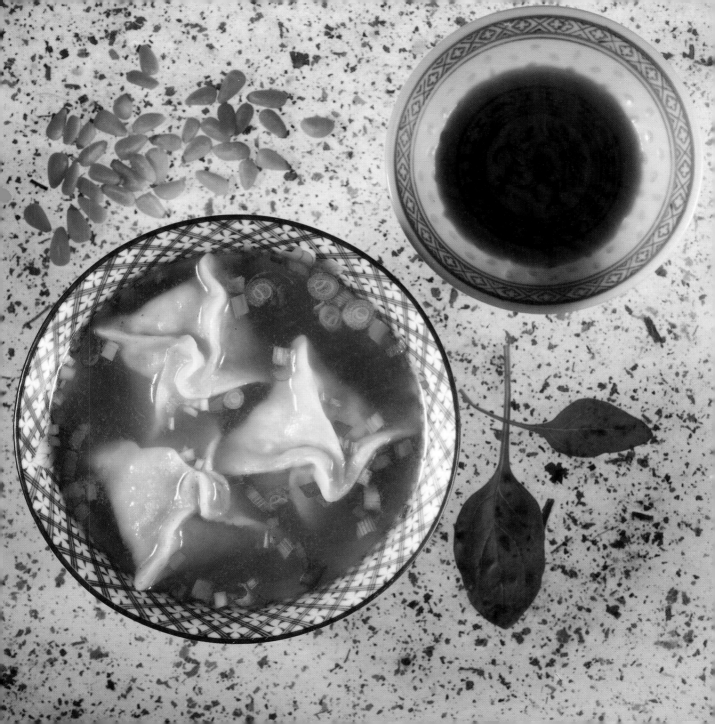

CORN & LENTIL SOUP

This pale-colored soup is made with corn and green lentils, and is similar in style to the traditional corn and crab-meat soup on page 27.

STEP 1

SERVES 4

2 tbsp green lentils
4 cups vegetable stock
1/2-inch piece gingerroot, finely chopped
2 tsp soy sauce
1 tsp sugar
1 tbsp cornstarch
3 tbsp dry sherry
11-oz can corn
1 egg white
1 tsp sesame oil
salt and pepper

TO GARNISH:
strips scallion
strips red chili

1 Wash the lentils in a strainer. Place in a saucepan with the stock, gingerroot, soy sauce and sugar. Bring to a boil and boil rapidly, uncovered, for 10 minutes. Skim off any froth on the surface. Reduce the heat, cover and simmer for 15 minutes.

2 Mix the cornstarch with the sherry in a small bowl. Add the corn with the liquid from the can and cornstarch mixture to the saucepan. Simmer over a low heat for 2 minutes, stirring occasionally.

3 Beat the egg white lightly with the sesame oil. Pour the egg mixture into the soup in a thin stream, remove from the heat and stir. The egg white will form white strands.

4 Season to taste. Pour into 4 warmed soup bowls and garnish with strips of scallion and chili before serving.

STEP 2

STEP 3

USING CANNED LENTILS

As a time-saver use a 14-oz can of green lentils instead of dried ones. Place the lentils and corn together in a large saucepan with the stock and flavorings, bring to a boil and simmer for 2 minutes, then continue the recipe from step 2. There is no need to boil canned lentils rapidly for 10 minutes.

STEP 3

STEP 1

STEP 3

STEP 4

STEP 5

MUSHROOM & CUCUMBER NOODLE SOUP

A light, refreshing clear soup of mushrooms, cucumber and small pieces of rice noodles, flavored with soy sauce and a touch of garlic.

SERVES 4

4 oz flat or open-cup mushrooms
$^1/_2$ English cucumber
2 scallions
1 garlic clove
2 tbsp vegetable oil
$^1/_4$ cup Chinese rice noodles
$^3/_4$ tsp salt
1 tbsp soy sauce

1 Wash the mushrooms and slice them thinly. Do not remove the peel as this adds more flavor. Halve the cucumber lengthwise. Scoop out the seeds, using a teaspoon, and slice the cucumber thinly.

2 Chop the scallions finely and cut the garlic clove into thin strips.

3 Heat the oil in a preheated wok or large saucepan. Add the scallions and garlic, and stir-fry for 30 seconds. Add the mushrooms and stir-fry for 2–3 minutes.

4 Stir in 2$^1/_2$ cups water. Break the noodles into short lengths and add to the soup. Bring to a boil over a high heat.

5 Add the cucumber slices, salt and soy sauce, stirring cccasionally.

6 Serve the soup in warmed bowls, distributing the noodles and vegetables evenly.

CUCUMBER SEEDS

Scooping the seeds out from the cucumber gives it a prettier effect when sliced, and also helps to reduce any bitterness, but if you prefer, you can leave them in.

STEP 1

STEP 2

STEP 3

STEP 4

LETTUCE & TOFU SOUP

This is a delicate, clear soup of shredded lettuce and small chunks of tofu with sliced carrot and scallion.

SERVES 4

7 oz tofu
2 tbsp vegetable oil
1 carrot, sliced thinly
¹/₂-inch piece gingerroot, cut into thin shreds
3 scallions, sliced diagonally
5 cups vegetable stock
2 tbsp soy sauce
2 tbsp dry sherry
1 tsp sugar
1¹/₂ cups romaine lettuce, shredded
salt and pepper

1 Cut the tofu into small cubes. Heat the oil in a preheated wok or large saucepan. Add the tofu and stir-fry until browned. Remove with a perforated spoon and drain on paper towels.

2 Add the carrot, gingerroot and scallions to the wok or saucepan and stir-fry for 2 minutes.

3 Add the stock, soy sauce, sherry and sugar. Bring to a boil and simmer for 1 minute.

4 Add the lettuce and stir until it has just wilted.

5 Return the tofu to the pan to reheat. Season with salt and pepper and serve in warmed bowls.

DECORATIVE CARROTS

For a prettier effect, score grooves along the length of the carrot with a sharp knife before slicing. This will create a flower effect as the carrot is cut into rounds. You could also try slicing the carrot on the diagonal to make longer slices. Try garnishing the soup with carrot curls – very fine strips of carrot that have been placed in iced water to make them curl up.

CHAPTER EIGHT

Main Meals

An abundance of high-quality produce can be bought from the markets in the towns and villages of China, and fresh food is purchased daily by endless streams of people buying the freshest goods for their family meals.

The simplest meal has a central dish of rice or noodles with a stir-fry or steamed dumplings, all of which are served at the same time, quite different from our Western way of eating. When entertaining, choose several different dishes to give as much variety of taste as possible, and prepare as much as you can in advance to enable you to spend more time with your guests than in the kitchen.

The following recipes contain ingredients that blend together to achieve a balanced contrast in color, flavor and texture. They are quick to prepare and cook. All the recipes in this section may be served as main courses with an accompaniment of rice or noodles.

Opposite: *One of the wonders of the world – the Great Wall of China.*

STEP 1

STEP 3

STEP 4

STEP 5

VEGETABLE & NUT STIR-FRY

A colorful selection of vegetables are stir-fried in a creamy peanut sauce and sprinkled with nuts to serve.

SERVES 4

3 tbsp crunchy peanut butter
²/₃ cup water
1 tbsp soy sauce
1 tsp sugar
1 carrot
¹/₂ red onion
4 baby zucchini
1 red bell pepper
8 oz egg thread noodles
¹/₄ cup peanuts, roughly chopped
2 tbsp vegetable oil
1 tsp sesame oil
1 small green chili, seeded and thinly sliced
1 garlic clove, thinly sliced
7¹/₂-oz can water chestnuts, rinsed, drained and sliced
3 cups bean sprouts
salt

1 Blend the peanut butter with the water gradually in a small bowl. Stir in the soy sauce and sugar.

2 Cut the carrot into thin matchsticks and slice the onion. Slice the zucchini on the diagonal and cut the bell pepper into even chunks.

3 Bring a large pan of water to a boil and add the egg noodles. Remove from the heat immediately and let rest for 4 minutes, stirring occasionally to divide the noodles.

4 Heat a preheated wok or large skillet. Add the peanuts and dry-fry until they are beginning to brown. Remove and set aside.

5 Add the oils to the pan and heat. Add the carrot, onion, zucchini, bell pepper, chili and garlic, and stir-fry for 2–3 minutes. Add the water chestnuts, bean sprouts and peanut sauce. Bring to a boil and heat thoroughly. Season to taste. Drain the noodles and serve with the stir-fry. Sprinkle with the peanuts.

VARIATION

The vegetables in this dish can be varied according to your taste and their availability. Make sure you choose a variety of colors for the best effect.

STEP 1

STEP 2

STEP 3

STEP 4

EGGPLANT IN BLACK BEAN SAUCE

Stir-fried eggplant is served in a black bean sauce with garlic and scallions. This would go well with rice and another vegetable dish such as stir-fried baby corn and green beans.

SERVES 4

generous ⅓ cup dried black beans
scant 2 cups vegetable stock
1 tbsp malt vinegar
1 tbsp dry sherry
1 tbsp soy sauce
1 tbsp sugar
1½ tsp cornstarch
1 red chili, seeded and chopped
½-inch piece gingerroot, chopped
2 eggplants
2 tsp salt
3 tbsp vegetable oil
2 garlic cloves, sliced
4 scallions, cut diagonally
shredded radishes, to garnish

1 Soak the beans overnight in plenty of cold water. Drain and place in a saucepan. Cover with cold water, bring to a boil and boil rapidly, uncovered, for 10 minutes. Drain. Return the beans to the saucepan with the stock and bring to a boil.

2 Blend together the vinegar, sherry, soy sauce, sugar, cornstarch, chili and ginger in a small bowl. Add to the saucepan, cover and simmer for 40 minutes, or until the beans are tender and the sauce thickens. Stir occasionally.

3 Cut the eggplants into chunks and place in a colander. Sprinkle over the salt and let drain for 30 minutes. Rinse well to remove the salt and dry on paper towels.

4 Heat the oil in a preheated wok or large skillet. Add the eggplant and garlic. Stir-fry for 3–4 minutes until the eggplant has started to brown.

5 Add the sauce to the eggplant chunks with the scallions. Heat thoroughly and garnish with radish shreds.

TIME-SAVER

To save time, you can use a bottled black bean sauce instead of making your own. You will need about 6 tablespoonfuls.

STIR-FRIED MUSHROOMS, CUCUMBER & SMOKED TOFU

Chunks of cucumber and smoked tofu stir-fried with straw mushrooms, snow peas and corn in a yellow bean sauce.

STEP 1

SERVES 4

1 large English cucumber
1 tsp salt
7½ oz smoked tofu
2 tbsp vegetable oil
2 oz snow peas
8 baby corn
1 celery stalk, sliced diagonally
14-oz can straw mushrooms, rinsed and
   drained
2 scallions, cut into strips
½-inch piece gingerroot, chopped
1 tbsp yellow bean sauce
1 tbsp light soy sauce
1 tbsp dry sherry

1 Halve the cucumber lengthwise. Remove the seeds, using a teaspoon. Cut into cubes, place in a colander and sprinkle over the salt. Let drain for 10 minutes. Rinse thoroughly in cold water to remove the salt and drain thoroughly.

2 Cut the tofu into cubes. Heat the oil in a preheated wok or large skillet. Add the tofu, snow peas, baby corn and celery. Stir until the tofu is lightly browned.

3 Add the straw mushrooms, scallions and ginger, and stir-fry for a further minute.

4 Stir in the cucumber, yellow bean sauce, soy sauce, sherry and 2 tablespoons water.

5 Continue to stir-fry for 1 minute more, then transfer to a serving plate and serve at once.

STEP 2

STEP 3

STRAW MUSHROOMS

Straw mushrooms are available in cans from Oriental suppliers and some supermarkets. If unavailable, substitute 8 oz baby button mushrooms.

STEP 4

STEP 2

STEP 3

STEP 4

STEP 6

VEGETABLE CASSEROLE WITH BLACK BEANS

This colorful Chinese-style casserole is made with tofu, vegetables and black bean sauce.

SERVES 4

6 Chinese dried mushrooms (if unavailable, use thinly sliced open-cup mushrooms)
9 oz tofu
3 tbsp vegetable oil
1 carrot, cut into thin strips
4 oz snow peas
8 baby corn, halved lengthwise
7½-oz can sliced bamboo shoots, rinsed and drained
1 red bell pepper, cored, seeded and cut into chunks
1½ cups Chinese leaves, shredded
1 tbsp soy sauce
1 tbsp black bean sauce
1 tsp sugar
1 tsp cornstarch
vegetable oil for deep-frying
8 oz Chinese rice noodles
salt

1 Place the dried mushrooms in a small bowl and cover with warm water. Let soak for 20–25 minutes. Drain and squeeze out the excess water, reserving the liquid. Remove the tough centers and slice the mushrooms thinly.

2 Cut the tofu into cubes. Boil in a saucepan of lightly salted water for 2–3 minutes to firm. Drain thoroughly.

3 Heat half the oil in a large flameproof casserole or saucepan. Add the tofu and fry until lightly browned all over. Remove with a perforated spoon and drain well on paper towels.

4 Add the remaining oil and stir-fry the mushrooms, carrot, snow peas, baby corn, bamboo shoots and bell pepper for 2–3 minutes. Add the Chinese leaves and tofu, and stir-fry for a further 2 minutes.

5 Stir in the soy sauce, black bean sauce and sugar, and season with salt. Add 6 tablespoons of the reserved mushroom liquid (or water if you are using ordinary mushrooms), mixed with cornstarch. Bring to a boil, reduce the heat, cover and braise for 2–3 minutes until the sauce has thickened slightly.

6 Heat the oil for deep-frying in a large saucepan. Add the noodles in batches and deep-fry until puffed up and lightly golden. Drain on paper towels and serve with the casserole.

STEP 2

STEP 5

STEP 5

STEP 6

MONEY BAGS

These traditional steamed dumplings are made with a mushroom and corn filling. Eat them as they are, or try dipping them in a mixture of soy sauce, sherry and slivers of gingerroot.

SERVES 4

*3 Chinese dried mushrooms (if unavailable,
  use thinly sliced open-cup mushrooms)
2 cups all-purpose flour
1 egg, beaten
6 tbsp water
1 tsp baking powder
³/₄ tsp salt
2 tbsp vegetable oil
2 scallions, chopped
¹/₂ cup corn kernels
¹/₂ red chili, seeded and chopped
1 tbsp brown bean sauce*

1 Place the dried mushrooms in a small bowl, cover with warm water and let soak for 20–25 minutes.

2 To make the wrappers, sift the flour into a bowl. Add the egg and mix in lightly. Stir in the water, baking powder and salt. Mix to make a soft dough. Knead lightly until smooth on a floured board. Cover with a damp cloth and set aside for 5–6 minutes. This allows the baking powder time to activate, so that the dumplings swell when steaming.

3 Drain the mushrooms, squeezing them dry. Remove the tough centers and chop the mushrooms.

4 Heat the oil in a preheated wok or large skillet. Add the mushrooms, scallions, corn and chili. Stir-fry for 2 minutes. Stir in the brown bean sauce and remove from the heat.

5 Roll the dough into a large sausage and cut into 24 even-sized pieces. Roll each piece out into a thin round and place a teaspoonful of the filling in the center. Gather up the edges to a point, pinch together and twist to seal.

6 Stand the dumplings in an oiled steaming basket. Place over a saucepan of simmering water, cover and steam for 12–14 minutes before serving.

COOKING WITH CABBAGE LEAVES

For extra flavor and to help to prevent the dumplings falling through the steamer, place them on cabbage leaves inside the steamer.

CARROTS & PARSNIPS WITH COCONUT

Sliced carrots and chunks of parsnip are cooked in a creamy coconut sauce with ground almonds and served on a bed of spinach.

STEP 1

SERVES 2

$^1/_3$ cup creamed coconut
$1^1/_4$ cups hot water
2 tbsp slivered almonds
4 tbsp vegetable oil
5 cardamom pods
4 thin slices gingerroot
$2^1/_2$ cups carrots, sliced
$2^1/_2$ cups parsnips, cored and cut into small chunks
$^1/_4$ tsp five-spice powder
2 tbsp ground almonds
4 cups young spinach leaves
$^1/_2$ red onion, thinly sliced
1 garlic clove, sliced
salt

1 Crumble the creamed coconut into a bowl or jug, add the hot water and stir until dissolved.

2 Heat a saucepan and dry-fry the slivered almonds until golden. Remove and set aside.

3 Heat half the oil in the saucepan. Add the cardamom pods and gingerroot. Fry for 30 seconds to flavor the oil. Add the carrots and parsnips. Stir-fry for 2–3 minutes.

4 Stir in the five-spice powder and ground almonds, and pour in the coconut liquid. Bring to a boil and season with salt to taste. Cover and simmer for 12–15 minutes until the vegetables are tender. Stir occasionally, adding extra water if necessary.

5 Wash the spinach and drain thoroughly. Remove any stems. Heat the remaining oil in a preheated wok or large skillet. Add the onion and garlic and stir-fry for 2 minutes. Add the spinach and stir-fry until it has just wilted. Drain off any excess liquid that has formed. Season with salt.

6 Remove the cardamom pods and gingerroot from the carrots and parsnips, and adjust the seasoning. Serve on a bed of the spinach sprinkled with the almonds.

STEP 3

STEP 4

CARDAMOM

Lightly crush the cardamom pods before using, as this helps to release their flavor.

STEP 5

STEP 1

STEP 2

STEP 4

STEP 5

LENTIL BALLS WITH SWEET & SOUR SAUCE

Crisp golden lentil balls are served in a sweet and sour sauce with bell peppers and pineapple chunks.

SERVES 4

1 cup red lentils
scant 2 cups water
$^1/_2$ green chili, seeded and chopped
4 scallions, finely chopped
1 garlic clove, crushed
1 tsp salt
4 tbsp pineapple juice from can
1 egg, beaten
vegetable oil for deep-frying

SAUCE:
3 tbsp white wine vinegar
2 tbsp sugar
2 tbsp tomato paste
1 tsp sesame oil
1 tsp cornstarch
$^1/_2$ tsp salt
6 tbsp water
2 canned pineapple rings
2 tbsp vegetable oil
$^1/_2$ red bell pepper, cut into chunks
$^1/_2$ green bell pepper, cut into chunks

1 Wash the lentils, then place in a saucepan with the water and bring to a boil. Skim and boil rapidly for 10 minutes, uncovered. Reduce the heat and simmer for 5 minutes until you have a fairly dry mixture. Considerably less water is used to cook these lentils than is normally required, so take care they do not burn as they cook. Stir occasionally.

2 Remove from the heat and stir in the chili, scallions, garlic, salt and pineapple juice. Let cool for 10 minutes.

3 To make the sauce, mix together the vinegar, sugar, tomato paste, sesame oil, cornstarch, salt and water, and set aside. Cut the pineapple into chunks.

4 Add the beaten egg to the lentil mixture. Heat the oil in a large saucepan or wok and deep-fry tablespoonfuls of the mixture in batches until crisp and golden. Remove with a perforated spoon and drain well on several layers of paper towels.

5 Heat the 2 tablespoons oil in a wok or skillet. Stir-fry the bell peppers for 2 minutes. Add the sauce mixture with the pineapple chunks. Bring to a boil, then reduce the heat and simmer for 1 minute, stirring constantly, until the sauce has thickened. Add the lentil balls and heat thoroughly, taking care not to break them up. Serve with rice or noodles.

CHAPTER NINE

Vegetables & Salads

Due to the vast size of China, in which there are many different climates, the country produces a huge variety of vegetables. These play a significant role in the Chinese diet, and are considered important in their own right rather than as mere accompaniments.

Many Westerners overcook their vegetables, boiling them in too much water and causing them to lose all their flavors and colors as well as their valuable vitamins and minerals. Stir-frying was until recently a method of cooking unique to the Chinese. The raw ingredients are cooked quickly with a minimum of oil or water over a high heat. This ensures that flavors, colors and nutrients are preserved leaving the vegetables crisp and colorful.

A mixture of raw and cooked vegetables is often used in Chinese salads, and these are picked fresh as they are needed. Choose firm crisp vegetables and cook them while they are at their best, as this will make all the difference to your final dish.

Opposite: *A tempting array of fresh fruits and vegetables in the western district of Hong Kong.*

STEP 1

STEP 2

STEP 4

STEP 5

EGGPLANT IN CHILI SAUCE

Strips of eggplant are deep-fried, then served in a fragrant chili sauce with carrot matchsticks and scallions.

SERVES 4

1 large eggplant
vegetable oil for deep-frying
2 carrots
4 scallions
2 large garlic cloves
1 tbsp vegetable oil
2 tsp chili sauce
1 tbsp soy sauce
1 tbsp dry sherry

1 Slice the eggplant and then cut into strips about the size of French fries.

2 Heat enough oil in a large heavy-based saucepan to deep-fry the eggplant in batches until just browned. Remove the strips with a perforated spoon and drain them on paper towels.

3 Cut the carrots into thin matchsticks. Trim and slice the scallions diagonally. Slice the garlic cloves.

4 Heat 1 tablespoon oil in a wok or large skillet. Add the carrot matchsticks and stir-fry for 1 minute, then add the chopped scallions and garlic and stir-fry for a further minute.

5 Stir in the chili sauce, soy sauce and sherry, then stir in the drained eggplant strips. Mix well to ensure that the vegetables are heated through thoroughly before serving.

MILDER FLAVOR

For a milder dish, substitute hoi-sin sauce for the chili sauce. This can be bought ready-made from all supermarkets.

STEP 1

STEP 2

STEP 3

STEP 4

GINGERED BROCCOLI WITH ORANGE

Thinly sliced broccoli flowerets are lightly stir-fried and served in a ginger and orange sauce.

SERVES 4

1 1/2 lb broccoli
2 thin slices gingerroot
2 garlic cloves
1 orange
2 tsp cornstarch
1 tbsp light soy sauce
1/2 tsp sugar
2 tbsp vegetable oil

1 Divide the broccoli into small flowerets. Peel the stems, using a vegetable peeler, and then cut them into thin slices. Cut the gingerroot into matchsticks and slice the garlic.

2 Peel 2 long strips of rind from the orange and cut into thin strips. Place the strips in a bowl, cover with cold water and set aside. Squeeze the juice from the orange and mix with the cornstarch, soy sauce, sugar and 4 tablespoons water.

3 Heat the oil in a wok or large skillet. Add the broccoli stem slices and stir-fry for 2 minutes. Add the gingerroot slices, garlic and broccoli flowerets, and stir-fry for a further 3 minutes.

4 Stir in the orange sauce mixture and cook, stirring constantly, until the sauce has thickened and coated the broccoli.

5 Drain the reserved orange rind and stir in before serving.

VARIATION

This dish could be made with cauliflower, if you prefer, or a mixture of cauliflower and broccoli.

LEMON CHINESE LEAVES

*These stir-fried Chinese leaves are served with a tangy sauce made of
grated lemon rind, lemon juice and ginger.*

STEP 1

SERVES 4

1 lb Chinese leaves
3 tbsp vegetable oil
1/2-inch piece gingerroot, grated
1 tsp salt
1 tsp sugar
1/2 cup water or vegetable stock
1 tsp grated lemon rind
1 tbsp cornstarch
1 tbsp lemon juice

1 Separate the Chinese leaves,
wash and drain thoroughly.
Pat dry with paper towels and then cut
into 2-inch wide slices.

2 Heat the oil in a preheated wok or
large skillet. Add the grated
gingerroot, followed by the Chinese
leaves. Stir-fry for 2–3 minutes or until
the leaves begin to wilt. Add the salt and
sugar, and mix well until the leaves
soften. Remove the leaves with a
perforated spoon and set aside.

3 Add the water or vegetable stock to
the pan with the grated lemon rind
and bring to a boil. Meanwhile, mix the
cornstarch to a smooth paste with the
lemon juice, then add to the water or
stock in the pan. Simmer, stirring

constantly, for about 1 minute to make a
smooth sauce.

4 Return the cooked leaves to the
pan and mix thoroughly. Arrange
on a serving plate and serve immediately.

STEP 2

STEP 3

CHINESE LEAVES

If Chinese leaves are unavailable,
substitute slices of savoy cabbage. Cook
for 1 extra minute to soften the leaves.

STEP 4

STEP 1

STEP 2

STEP 3

STEP 4

GOLDEN NEEDLES WITH BAMBOO SHOOTS

Golden needles are the dried flower buds of the tiger lily. They are usually sold in the dried form and can be obtained from specialist Chinese stores. They give a unique musky flavor to this dish.

SERVES 4

1/4 *cup dried lily flowers*
2 × 7 1/2-*oz cans bamboo shoots, rinsed and drained*
1/2 *cup cornstarch*
vegetable oil for deep-frying
1 tbsp vegetable oil
scant 2 cups vegetable stock
1 tbsp dark soy sauce
1 tbsp dry sherry
1 tsp sugar
1 large garlic clove, sliced
1/2 *each red, green and yellow bell peppers*

1 Soak the lily flowers in hot water for 30 minutes.

2 Coat the bamboo shoots in cornstarch. Heat enough oil in a large heavy-based saucepan to deep-fry the bamboo shoots in batches until just beginning to color. Remove with a perforated spoon and drain on paper towels.

3 Drain the lily flowers and trim off the hard ends. Heat 1 tablespoon oil in a wok or large skillet. Add the lily flowers, bamboo shoots, stock, soy sauce, sherry, sugar and garlic.

4 Slice the bell peppers thinly and add to the pan. Bring to a boil, stirring constantly, then reduce the heat and simmer for 5 minutes. Add extra water or stock if necessary.

COATING THE · BAMBOO SHOOTS

To coat the bamboo shoots easily with cornstarch, place the cornstarch in a plastic bag, add the bamboo shoots in batches and shake well.

STEP 1

STEP 3

STEP 4

STEP 5

SPINACH WITH STRAW MUSHROOMS

Straw mushrooms are available in cans from Oriental stores. Here they are served with spinach, raisins and pine nuts. You can use button mushrooms instead, if straw mushrooms are unavailable.

SERVES 4

$^1\!/_4$ cup pine nuts
1 lb fresh spinach leaves
3 tbsp vegetable oil
1 red onion, sliced
2 garlic cloves, sliced
14-oz can straw mushrooms, rinsed and
    drained
3 tbsp raisins
2 tbsp soy sauce
salt

1 Heat a wok or large skillet and dry-fry the pine nuts until lightly browned. Remove and set aside.

2 Wash the spinach thoroughly, picking the leaves over and removing long stems. Drain and pat dry with paper towels.

3 Heat the oil in the preheated wok or skillet. Add the onion and garlic, and stir-fry for 1 minute.

4 Add the spinach and mushrooms, and continue to stir-fry until the leaves have wilted. Drain off all the excess liquid.

5 Stir in the raisins, reserved pine nuts and soy sauce. Stir-fry until thoroughly heated and well-mixed. Season to taste with salt before serving.

ADDING FLAVOR

Soak the raisins in 2 tablespoons dry sherry before using. This helps to plump them up as well as adding extra flavor to the stir-fry.

GADO GADO SALAD

This salad is a mixture of cooked and raw vegetables in a spicy peanut dressing. The vegetables can either be arranged in individual piles on the serving platter or mixed together.

STEP 2

SERVES 4

8 oz new potatoes, scrubbed
4 oz green beans
4 oz cauliflower, broken into small flowerets
1½ cups white cabbage, shredded
1 carrot, cut into thin sticks
¼ English cucumber, cut into chunks
2 cups bean sprouts
2 hard-cooked eggs

SAUCE:
6 tbsp crunchy peanut butter
1¼ cups cold water
1 garlic clove, crushed
1 fresh red chili, seeded and finely chopped
2 tbsp soy sauce
1 tbsp dry sherry
2 tsp sugar
1 tbsp lemon juice

1 Halve the potatoes and place in a saucepan of lightly salted water. Bring to a boil and then simmer for 12–15 minutes or until cooked through, whichever is the sooner. Drain and plunge into cold water to cool.

2 Bring another pan of lightly salted water to a boil. Add the green beans, cauliflower and cabbage, and cook for 3 minutes. Drain and plunge the vegetables into cold water to cool and prevent any further cooking.

3 Drain the potatoes and other cooked vegetables. Arrange in piles on a large serving platter with the carrot, cucumber and bean-sprouts.

4 Remove the shells from the hard-cooked eggs, cut into quarters and arrange on the salad. Cover and set aside.

5 To make the sauce, place the peanut butter in a bowl and blend in the water gradually, followed by the remaining ingredients.

6 Uncover the salad, place the sauce in a separate serving bowl and drizzle some over each serving.

STEP 3

STEP 4

COCONUT MILK

For extra flavor in the peanut sauce, use coconut milk instead of water. This can be purchased from specialist Oriental stores and some supermarkets.

STEP 5

STEP 1

STEP 2

STEP 3

STEP 4

ORIENTAL SALAD

This colorful crisp salad has a fresh orange dressing and is topped with crunchy vermicelli.

SERVES 4–6

1/4 cup dried vermicelli
1/2 head Chinese leaves
2 cups bean sprouts
6 radishes
4 oz snow peas
1 large carrot
4 oz sprouting beans

DRESSING:
juice of 1 orange
1 tbsp sesame seeds, toasted
1 tsp honey
1 tsp sesame oil
1 tbsp hazelnut oil

1 Break the vermicelli into small strands. Heat a wok or skillet and dry-fry the vermicelli until lightly golden. Remove from the pan and set aside.

2 Shred the Chinese leaves and wash with the bean sprouts. Drain thoroughly and place in a large bowl. Slice the radishes. Trim the snow peas and cut each into 3 pieces. Cut the carrot into thin matchsticks. Add the sprouting beans and prepared vegetables to the bowl.

3 Place all the dressing ingredients in a screw-top jar and shake until well-blended. Pour over the salad and toss together well.

4 Transfer the salad to a serving bowl and sprinkle over the reserved vermicelli before serving.

SPROUTING BEANS

If you are unable to buy sprouting beans, you can make your own. Use a mixture of mung and aduki beans and garbanzo beans. Soak the beans overnight in cold water, drain and rinse. Place in a large glass jam jar and cover the mouth of the jar with a piece of cheesecloth tied on to secure it. Lay the jar on its side and place in indirect light. For the next 2–3 days rinse the beans once each day in cold water until they are ready to eat.

CHAPTER TEN

Rice & Noodles

Rice and noodles form the central part of most Oriental meals, particularly in the southern part of China. In the north the staple foods tend to contain more wheat-based products, such as dumplings. Rice and noodles supply the carbohydrate necessary for a nutritious meal, and though bland in themselves they provide a complementary texture to the other ingredients and absorb the stronger flavors of other dishes, making them an essential and very satisfying part of the Chinese meal.

The most common types of rice used in Chinese cuisine include white or brown long-grain rice and glutinous rice. The shorter grain of the glutinous rice has a slight stickiness when cooked, which makes it ideal for eating with chopsticks.

Rice can be boiled and then steamed, or it can be fried with other ingredients added, such as scrambled eggs, scallions or peas, then flavored with soy sauce. It is also used to make wines, vinegars, noodles and flour, which makes it a very important ingredient.

A wide variety of Chinese noodles are available, made from wheat, buckwheat or rice flours. Like rice, they are very versatile; they can be boiled or fried, and served plain with a sauce, or in a soup.

Opposite: *A 1000-year old banyan tree overhangs a rice field in the Guangxi province.*

STEP 1

STEP 3

STEP 4

STEP 5

HOMEMADE NOODLES WITH STIR-FRIED VEGETABLES

These noodles are simple to make; you do not need a pasta-making machine as they are rolled out by hand.

SERVES 2–4

NOODLES:
1 cup all-purpose flour
2 tbsp cornstarch
$^1/_2$ tsp salt
$^1/_2$ cup boiling water
5 tbsp vegetable oil

STIR-FRY:
1 zucchini
1 celery stalk
1 carrot
4 oz open-cup mushrooms
1 leek
4 oz broccoli
2 cups bean sprouts
1 tbsp soy sauce
2 tsp rice wine vinegar (if unavailable, use
    white wine vinegar)
$^1/_2$ tsp sugar

1 To prepare the noodles, sift the flour, cornstarch and salt into a bowl. Make a well in the center and pour in the boiling water and 1 teaspoon of the oil. Mix quickly, using a wooden spoon, to make a soft dough. Cover and leave for 5–6 minutes.

2 Prepare the vegetables for the stir-fry. Cut the zucchini, celery and carrot into thin sticks. Slice the mushrooms and leek. Divide the broccoli into small flowerets and peel and thinly slice the stems.

3 Make the noodles by breaking off small pieces of dough and rolling into balls. Then roll each ball across a very lightly oiled counter with the palm of your hand to form thin noodles. Do not worry if some of the noodles break into shorter lengths. Set the noodles aside.

4 Heat 3 tablespoons of oil in a wok or large skillet. Add the noodles in batches and fry over a high heat for 1 minute. Reduce the heat and cook for a further 2 minutes. Remove and drain on paper towels. Set aside.

5 Heat the remaining oil in the pan. Add the zucchini, celery and carrot, and stir-fry for 1 minute. Add the mushrooms, broccoli and leek, and stir-fry for a further minute. Stir in the remaining ingredients and mix well until thoroughly heated.

6 Add the noodles and toss to mix together over a high heat. Serve immediately.

STEP 2

STEP 3

STEP 4

STEP 5

VEGETABLE CHOW MEIN

Egg noodles are fried with a colorful variety of vegetables to make this well-known dish.

SERVES 4

1 lb egg noodles
4 tbsp vegetable oil
1 onion, thinly sliced
2 carrots, cut into thin sticks
1⅓ cups button mushrooms, quartered
4 oz snow peas
½ English cucumber, cut into sticks
2 cups spinach, shredded
2 cups bean sprouts
2 tbsp dark soy sauce
1 tbsp sherry
1 tsp salt
1 tsp sugar
1 tsp cornstarch
1 tsp sesame oil

1 Cook the noodles according to the package instructions. Drain and rinse under running cold water until cool. Set aside.

2 Heat 3 tablespoons of the vegetable oil in a wok or large skillet. Add the onion and carrots, and stir-fry for 1 minute. Add the mushroom quarters, snow peas and cucumber, and stir-fry for a further 1 minute.

3 Stir in the remaining vegetable oil and then add the drained noodles together with the spinach and bean sprouts.

4 Blend together the remaining ingredients and pour over the noodles and vegetables.

5 Stir-fry until thoroughly heated and serve.

FOR A HOTTER FLAVOR

For a spicy hot chow mein, add 1 tablespoon chili sauce or substitute chili oil for the sesame oil.

144

VEGETARIAN FRIED RICE

In this simple recipe, cooked rice is fried with vegetables and cashew nuts. It can either be eaten on its own or served as an accompaniment.

STEP 2

SERVES 2–4

generous ³/₄ cup long-grain rice
¹/₂ cup cashew nuts
1 carrot
¹/₂ English cucumber
1 yellow bell pepper
2 scallions
2 tbsp vegetable oil
1 garlic clove, crushed
³/₄ cup frozen peas, defrosted
1 tbsp soy sauce
1 tsp salt
cilantro leaves, to garnish

1 Bring a large pan of water to a boil. Add the rice and simmer for 15 minutes. Tip the rice into a strainer and rinse; drain thoroughly.

2 Heat a wok or large skillet. Add the cashew nuts and dry-fry until lightly browned. Remove and set aside.

3 Cut the carrot in half along the length, then slice thinly into semi-circles. Halve the cucumber and remove the seeds, using a teaspoon; dice the cucumber. Slice the bell pepper and chop the scallions.

4 Heat the oil in the wok or large skillet. Add the prepared vegetables and the garlic. Stir-fry for 3 minutes. Add the rice, peas, soy sauce and salt. Continue to stir-fry until well mixed and thoroughly heated.

5 Stir in the reserved cashew nuts and serve garnished with cilantro leaves.

STEP 3

STEP 4

LAST-MINUTE MEAL

You can replace any of the vegetables in this recipe with others suitable for a stir-fry, and using leftover rice makes this a perfect last-minute dish.

STEP 4

STEP 1

STEP 4

STEP 5

STEP 6

FRAGRANT STEAMED RICE IN LOTUS LEAVES

The fragrance of the leaves penetrates the rice, giving it a unique taste. Lotus leaves can be bought from specialist Chinese stores. Large cabbage or spinach leaves can be used as a substitute.

SERVES 4

2 lotus leaves
4 Chinese dried mushrooms (if unavailable,
　use thinly sliced open-cup mushrooms)
generous ¾ cup long-grain rice
1 cinnamon stick
6 cardamom pods
4 cloves
1 tsp salt
2 eggs
1 tbsp vegetable oil
2 scallions, chopped
1 tbsp soy sauce
2 tbsp sherry
1 tsp sugar
1 tsp sesame oil

1 Unfold the lotus leaves carefully and cut along the fold to divide each leaf in half. Lay on a large baking tray and pour over enough hot water to cover. Let soak for about 30 minutes or until the leaves have softened.

2 Place the dried mushrooms in a small bowl and cover with warm water. Let soak for 20–25 minutes.

3 Cook the rice in plenty of boiling water in a saucepan with the cinnamon stick, cardamom pods, cloves and salt for about 10 minutes – the rice should be partially cooked. Drain thoroughly and remove the cinnamon.

4 Beat the eggs lightly. Heat the oil in a preheated wok or skillet and cook the eggs quickly, stirring constantly until they are set; then remove and set aside.

5 Drain the mushrooms, squeezing out the excess water. Remove the tough centers and chop the mushrooms. Place the rice in a bowl. Stir in the mushrooms, cooked egg, scallions, soy sauce, sherry, sugar and sesame oil. Season with salt to taste.

6 Drain the lotus leaves and divide the rice mixture into 4 portions. Place a portion in the center of each lotus leaf and fold up to form a package. Place in a steamer, cover and steam over simmering water for 20 minutes. To serve, cut the tops of the lotus leaves open to expose the fragrant rice inside.

STEP 1

STEP 2

STEP 3

STEP 5

SPICY COCONUT RICE WITH GREEN LENTILS

Rice and green lentils are cooked with creamed coconut, lemongrass and curry leaves. This recipe will serve two people as a main course or four as an accompaniment.

SERVES 2–4

$^1/_3$ cup green lentils
generous 1 cup long-grain rice
2 tbsp vegetable oil
1 onion, sliced
2 garlic cloves, crushed
3 curry leaves
1 stalk lemongrass, chopped (if unavailable,
    use grated rind of $^1/_2$ lemon)
1 green chili, seeded and chopped
$^1/_2$ tsp cumin seeds
$1^1/_2$ tsp salt
$^1/_3$ cup creamed coconut
$2^1/_2$ cups hot water
2 tbsp chopped fresh cilantro

TO GARNISH:
shredded radishes
shredded English cucumber

1 Wash the lentils and place in a saucepan. Cover with cold water, bring to a boil and boil rapidly for 10 minutes. Wash the rice thoroughly and drain well.

2 Heat the oil in a large saucepan, which has a tight-fitting lid, and fry the onion for 3–4 minutes. Add the garlic, curry leaves, lemongrass, chili, cumin seeds and salt, and stir well.

3 Drain the lentils and rinse. Add to the onion and spices with the rice and mix well. Add the creamed coconut to the hot water and stir until dissolved. Stir into the rice mixture and bring to a boil. Turn down the heat to low, put the lid on tightly and let cook undisturbed for 15 minutes.

4 Without removing the lid, remove the pan from the heat and let rest for 10 minutes to allow the rice and lentils to finish cooking in their own steam.

5 Stir in the cilantro and remove the curry leaves. Serve garnished with shredded radishes and cucumber.

CREAMED COCONUT

If creamed coconut is unavailable, use $^2/_3$ cup shredded coconut. Infuse it in the hot water for 20 minutes, drain well and squeeze out any excess water. Discard the coconut and use the liquid.

STEP 2

STEP 3

STEP 5

STEP 6

EGG FU-YUNG WITH RICE

In this dish, cooked rice is mixed with scrambled eggs, Chinese mushrooms, bamboo shoots and water chestnuts, and it is a great way of using up leftover cooked rice. It can be served as a meal by itself or as an accompaniment.

SERVES 2–4

generous ³/₄ cup long-grain rice
2 Chinese dried mushrooms (if unavailable,
    use thinly sliced open-cup mushrooms)
3 eggs, beaten
3 tbsp vegetable oil
4 scallions, sliced
¹/₂ green bell pepper, cored, seeded and
    chopped
¹/₃ cup canned bamboo shoots, rinsed and
    drained
¹/₃ cup canned water chestnuts, rinsed,
    drained and sliced
125 g/4 oz/2 cups bean sprouts
2 tbsp light soy sauce
2 tbsp dry sherry
2 tsp sesame oil
salt and pepper

1 Cook the rice in lightly salted boiling water according to the package instructions.

2 Place the dried mushrooms in a small bowl, cover with warm water and let soak for 20–25 minutes.

3 Mix the beaten eggs with a little salt. Heat 1 tablespoon of the oil in a wok or large skillet. Add the eggs and stir until just set. Remove and set aside.

4 Drain the mushrooms and squeeze out the excess water. Remove the tough centers and chop the mushrooms.

5 Heat the remaining oil in a clean wok or skillet. Add the mushrooms, scallions and green bell pepper, and stir-fry for 2 minutes. Add the bamboo shoots, water chestnuts and bean-sprouts. Stir-fry for 1 minute.

6 Drain the rice thoroughly and add to the pan with the remaining ingredients. Mix well, heating the rice thoroughly. Season to taste with salt and pepper. Stir in the reserved eggs and serve at once.

WASHING BEAN SPROUTS

To wash bean sprouts, place them in a bowl of cold water and swirl with your hand. Remove any long tail ends.

APPETIZERS

•

SOUPS

•

SEAFOOD DISHES

•

MEAT & POULTRY DISHES

•

VEGETABLES, RICE & NOODLES

3

**SZECHUAN
COOKING**

CHAPTER ELEVEN

Appetizers

Appetizers are often served as the first course or for nibbles with
drinks in Szechuan – just like hors d'oeuvres in the West.
The advantage of these dishes is that they can generally be
prepared and even cooked well in advance – hours before serving
if need be. Also, almost all the dishes selected here are ideal
for a buffet-style meal or as party food.

Instead of serving a selection of appetizers individually, you can
serve a small portion of several or all together as an assortment.
Select a minimum of three different items such as Deep-fried
Shrimp, Bang-bang Chicken, Deep-fried Spareribs
and so on.

Other dishes that can be served as a part of the appetizer selection
are Szechuan Shrimp, Sweet & Sour Shrimp, Aromatic & Crispy
Duck, and Braised Chinese Leaves. Remember not to have
more than one of the same type of food, and the ingredients should
be chosen for their harmony and balance in color,
aroma, flavor and texture.

Opposite: *The Great Wall
snakes across many miles of
this vast country.*

STEP 1

STEP 2

STEP 3

STEP 4

DEEP-FRIED SHRIMP

*For best results, use raw jumbo shrimp in their shells. They are
3–4 inches long, and you should get 18–20 shrimp per 1 lb.*

SERVES 4

*8–10 oz raw shrimp in their shells,
    defrosted if frozen
1 tbsp light soy sauce
1 tsp Chinese rice wine or dry sherry
2 tsp cornstarch
vegetable oil for deep-frying
2–3 scallions, to garnish*

*SPICY SALT AND PEPPER:
1 tbsp salt
1 tsp ground Szechuan peppercorns
1 tsp five-spice powder*

1 Pull the soft legs off the shrimp, but
keep the body shell on. Dry well on
paper towels.

2 Place the shrimp in a bowl with the
soy sauce, wine and cornstarch.
Turn to coat and let marinate for about
25–30 minutes.

3 To make the Spicy Salt and Pepper,
mix the salt, pepper and five-spice
powder together. Place in a dry skillet
and stir-fry for 3–4 minutes over a low
heat, stirring constantly. Remove from
the heat and let cool.

4 Heat the oil in a preheated wok
until smoking, then deep-fry the
shrimp in batches until golden brown.
Remove with a slotted spoon and drain
on paper towels.

5 Place the scallions in a bowl, pour
on 1 tablespoon of the hot oil and
leave for 30 seconds. Serve the shrimp
garnished with the scallions, and with
Spicy Salt and Pepper as a dip.

ROASTING SPICES

The roasted spice mixture made with
Szechuan peppercorns is used throughout
China as a dip for deep-fried food. The
peppercorns are sometimes roasted first
and then ground. Dry-frying is a way of
releasing the flavors of the spices. You can
make the dip in advance and store in a
tightly sealed jar until ready to use.

STEP 1

STEP 2

STEP 3

STEP 4

PORK WITH CHILI & GARLIC SAUCE

Any leftovers from this dish can be used for a number of other dishes –
such as Hot & Sour Soup (see page 170), and Twice-cooked Pork
(see page 203).

SERVES 4

1 lb leg of pork, boned but not skinned

SAUCE:
1 tsp finely chopped garlic
1 tsp finely chopped scallions
2 tbsp light soy sauce
1 tsp red chili oil
1/2 tsp sesame oil

1 Place the pork, tied together in one piece, in a large pan, add enough cold water to cover and bring to a rolling boil over a medium heat.

2 Skim off the scum that rises to the surface, cover and simmer slowly for 25–30 minutes.

3 Let the meat in the liquid cool, under cover, for at least 1–2 hours. Lift out the meat with 2 slotted spoons and let cool completely, skin-side up, for 2–3 hours.

4 To serve, cut off the skin from the pork, taking care to leave a very thin layer of fat on top like a ham joint. Next, cut the meat in small thin slices across the grain, and arrange the slices neatly on a plate. Mix together the sauce ingredients, and pour the sauce evenly over the pork.

SZECHUAN CHILI

One of the local Szechuan plants that contributes most to the typical character of the region's cooking is the small red fagara chili, which is used both fresh and dried. The chili has a delayed action on the palate; at first it seems to have little taste, but suddenly it burns the mouth with great ferocity, so it is used with much respect. It is claimed that instead of burning the taste-buds, the chili actually makes them more sensitive to other flavors.

This is a very simple dish, but beautifully presented. Make sure you slice the meat as thinly and evenly as possible to make an elegantly arranged dish.

BANG-BANG CHICKEN

The cooked chicken meat is tenderized by being beaten with a rolling pin, hence the name for this very popular Szechuan dish.

STEP 1

SERVES 4

4 cups water
2 chicken quarters (breast half and leg)
1 English cucumber, cut into matchstick
  shreds

SAUCE:
2 tbsp light soy sauce
1 tsp sugar
1 tbsp finely chopped scallions
1 tsp red chili oil
1/4 tsp pepper
1 tsp white sesame seeds
2 tbsp peanut butter, creamed with a little
  sesame oil

1 Bring the water to a rolling boil in a wok or a large pan. Add the chicken pieces, reduce the heat, cover and simmer for 30–35 minutes.

2 Remove the chicken from the pan and immerse it in a bowl of cold water for at least 1 hour to cool it, ready for shredding.

3 Remove the chicken pieces and drain well. Dry the chicken pieces on absorbent paper towels, then take the meat off the bone.

4 On a flat surface, pound the chicken with a rolling pin, then tear the meat into shreds with 2 forks. Mix with the shredded cucumber and arrange in a serving dish.

5 To serve, mix together all the sauce ingredients and pour over the chicken and cucumber.

STEP 2

STEP 4

STEP 4

THE CHOICEST CHICKEN

This dish is also known as Bon-bon Chicken – *bon* is a Chinese word for stick, so again the tenderizing technique inspires the recipe name.

Take the time to tear the chicken meat into similar-sized shreds, to make an elegant-looking dish. You can do this quite efficiently with 2 forks, although Chinese cooks would do it with their fingers.

STEP 1

STEP 1

STEP 2

STEP 3

PICKLED CUCUMBER

The pickling takes minutes rather than days – but the longer you leave it, the better the result. Some pickled vegetables are marinated for days – see the recipe for Mixed Pickled Vegetables, below.

SERVES 4

1 slender English cucumber, about
   12 inches long
1 tsp salt
2 tsp superfine sugar
1 tsp rice vinegar
1 tsp red chili oil
a few drops sesame oil

1 Halve the cucumber, unpeeled, lengthwise. Scrape off the seeds and cut across into thick chunks.

2 Sprinkle with the salt and mix well. Let marinate for at least 20–30 minutes, longer if possible, then pour the juice away.

3 Mix the cucumber with the sugar, vinegar and chili oil, and sprinkle with the sesame oil just before serving.

MIXED PICKLED VEGETABLES

12 oz Chinese leaves, cut into bite-sized
   pieces
2 oz green beans, topped and tailed
1 cup carrots, diced
3 chilies, seeded and finely chopped
2 tsp Szechuan peppercorns
2 tbsp kosher salt
2 tbsp rice wine

Place the vegetables in a glass bowl with the chilies, peppercorns, salt and wine. Stir well, cover and let marinate in the refrigerator for 4 days. Serve cold, as a salad.

PICKLED VEGETABLES

Pickled vegetables and fruits are very popular with the Chinese. They are often served as snacks and appetizers, and can also be served with cold meat dishes. Usually, the vegetables are allowed to stay in the marinade for 3–4 days. Once made, they will keep in the refrigerator for up to 2 weeks.

STEP 1

STEP 2

STEP 3

STEP 4

DEEP-FRIED SPARERIBS

The spareribs should be chopped into small bite-sized pieces before or after cooking.

SERVES 4

8–10 finger spareribs
1 tsp five-spice powder or 1 tbsp mild curry
* powder*
1 tbsp rice wine or dry sherry
1 egg
2 tbsp all-purpose flour
vegetable oil for deep-frying
1 tsp finely shredded scallions
1 tsp finely shredded fresh green or red hot
* chilies, seeded*
salt and pepper
Spicy Salt and Pepper (see page 158),
* to serve*

1 Chop the ribs into 3–4 small pieces. Place the ribs in a bowl with salt, pepper, five-spice or curry powder and the wine. Turn to coat the ribs in the spices and let them marinate for 1–2 hours.

2 Mix the egg and flour together to make a batter.

3 Dip the ribs in the batter one by one to coat well.

4 Heat the oil in a preheated wok until smoking. Deep-fry the ribs for 4–5 minutes, then remove with a slotted spoon and drain thoroughly on paper towels.

5 Reheat the oil over a high heat and deep-fry the ribs once more for another minute. Remove and drain again on paper towels.

6 Pour 1 tablespoon of the hot oil over the scallions and chilies and leave for 30–40 seconds. Serve the ribs with Spicy Salt and Pepper, garnished with the shredded scallions and chilies.

FINGER RIBS

To make finger ribs, cut the sheet of spareribs into individual ribs down each side of the bones. These ribs are then chopped into bite-sized pieces for deep-frying.

CHAPTER TWELVE

Soups

Soup is not normally served as a separate course in China, except at formal occasions and banquets, when it usually appears toward the end of the meal.

Otherwise, in Chinese homes a simply-made soup is served with all the other dishes throughout the meal. The soup is almost always a clear broth in which some thinly sliced vegetables and/or meat have been poached quickly.

The soup should ideally be made with a good stock. If you use a bouillon cube, remember to reduce the amount of seasoning in the recipes, since most commercially-made cubes are fairly salty and spicy. It is always worth while making your own Chinese stock, following the recipe on page 230, if you have the time.

Opposite: Fresh vegetables on display in a market in Szechuan. The Chinese shop daily in the markets to ensure that produce is absolutely fresh and crisp.

STEP 1

STEP 2

STEP 3

STEP 4

HOT & SOUR SOUP

This is the favorite soup in Chinese restaurants throughout the world.

SERVES 4

*4-6 dried Chinese mushrooms (shiitake),
   soaked
4 oz cooked pork or chicken
1 cake tofu
2 oz canned sliced bamboo shoots, rinsed and
   drained
2¹/₂ cups Chinese Stock (see page 230)
   or water
1 tbsp Chinese rice wine or dry sherry
1 tbsp light soy sauce
2 tbsp rice vinegar
1 tbsp cornstarch paste (see page 231)
salt, to taste
¹/₂ tsp ground white pepper
2-3 scallions, thinly sliced, to serve*

1 Drain the mushrooms, squeeze dry and discard the hard stems. Thinly slice the mushrooms.

2 Thinly slice the meat, tofu and bamboo shoots into narrow shreds.

3 Bring the stock or water to a rolling boil in a wok or large saucepan and add all the ingredients. Bring back to a boil, then simmer for about 1 minute.

4 Add the wine, soy sauce and vinegar and bring back to a boil

once more, stirring. Using a wooden spoon, stir in the cornstarch paste to thicken the soup. Serve hot, sprinkled with the thinly sliced scallions.

DRIED MUSHROOMS

There are many varieties of dried mushrooms, which add a particular flavor to Chinese cooking. Shiitake mushrooms are one of the favorite kinds to use. Soak in hot water for 25–30 minutes before use and cut off the hard stems.

If you strain the soaking liquid through fine cheesecloth, you can use the liquid to give a mushroom flavor to other soups, as well as sauces and casseroles. It is important to strain the liquid carefully because it will contain small, gritty particles.

STEP 1

STEP 1

STEP 2

STEP 3

THREE-FLAVOR SOUP

Ideally, use raw shrimp in this soup. If that is not possible, add ready-cooked ones at the very last stage.

SERVES 4

4 oz skinned, boned chicken breast
4 oz raw peeled shrimp
salt
¹/₂ egg white, lightly beaten
2 tsp cornstarch paste (see page 231)
4 oz honey-roast ham
3 cups Chinese Stock (see page 230)
   or water
finely chopped scallions, to garnish

1 Thinly slice the chicken into small shreds. If the shrimp are large, cut each in half lengthwise, otherwise leave whole. Place the chicken and shrimps in a bowl and mix with a pinch of salt, the egg white and cornstarch paste until well coated.

2 Cut the ham into small thin slices roughly the same size as the chicken pieces.

3 Bring the stock or water to a rolling boil, add the chicken, the raw shrimp and the ham. Bring the soup back to a boil, and simmer for 1 minute.

4 Adjust the seasoning and serve the soup hot, garnished with the scallions.

COOKING TIPS

Soups such as this are improved enormously in flavor if you use a well-flavored stock. Either use a bouillon cube, or find time to make Chinese Stock – see the recipe on page 230. Better still, make double quantities and freeze some for future use.

Fresh, uncooked shrimp impart the best flavor. If these are not available, you can use ready-cooked shrimp. They must be added at the last moment before serving to prevent them becoming tough and over-cooked.

STEP 1

STEP 2

STEP 3

STEP 4

PORK & SZECHUAN VEGETABLE

Sold in cans, Szechuan preserved vegetable is pickled mustard root which is quite hot and salty, so rinse in water before use.

SERVES 4

8 oz pork tenderloin
2 tsp cornstarch paste (see page 231)
4 oz Szechuan preserved vegetable
3 cups Chinese stock (see page 230)
  or water
salt and pepper
a few drops sesame oil (optional)
2–3 scallions, sliced, to garnish

1 Cut the pork across the grain into thin shreds and mix with the cornstarch paste.

2 Wash and rinse the Szechuan preserved vegetable, then cut into thin shreds the same size as the pork.

3 Bring the stock or water to a rolling boil. Add the pork and stir to separate the shreds. Return to a boil.

4 Add the Szechuan preserved vegetable and bring back to a boil once more. Adjust the seasoning and sprinkle with sesame oil. Serve hot, garnished with scallions.

SZECHUAN PRESERVED VEGETABLE

The Chinese are fond of pickles, and there are many varieties of pickled vegetables. In the Szechuan region, in particular, preserved vegetables are important because the region is over 1,000 miles from the coast. Vinegar and salt (from the province's extensive salt mines) are used to make a range of pickled foods, which are used in cooking and eaten on their own.

One of the most popular is Szechuan preserved vegetable, a speciality of the province, available in cans from specialist Chinese supermarkets. It is actually mustard green root, pickled in salt and chilies. It gives a crunchy, spicy taste to dishes. Rinse in cold water before use. Once opened the vegetable should be stored in a tightly sealed jar and kept in the refrigerator.

SPINACH & TOFU SOUP

This is a very colorful and delicious soup. If spinach is not in season, watercress or lettuce can be used instead.

STEP 1

SERVES 4

1 cake tofu
4 oz spinach leaves without stems
3 cups Chinese Stock (see page 230) or
    water
1 tbsp light soy sauce
salt and pepper

1 Cut the tofu into small pieces about ¹/₄ in thick. Wash the spinach leaves and cut them into small pieces or shreds, discarding any discolored leaves and tough stems. (If possible, use fresh young spinach leaves, which have not yet developed tough ribs. Otherwise, it is important to cut out all the ribs and stems for this soup.)

STEP 1

2 In a wok or large pan, bring the stock to a rolling boil. Add the tofu and soy sauce, bring back to a boil and simmer for about 2 minutes.

3 Add the spinach and simmer for 1 more minute.

4 Skim the surface of the soup to make it clear, adjust the seasoning and serve.

STEP 2

SERVING SUGGESTIONS

There is no set order of courses for Chinese meals. The soup is an integral part of the meal; it may be served first, but people can help themselves to more during the meal. The soup is usually presented in a large bowl placed in the center of the table, and consumed as the meal progresses. It serves as a refresher between different dishes and as a beverage throughout the meal. (Water is never served during the meal, and tea is brought only before and after a meal.)

Each person at the table has a bowl, rather than a plate, that is used for all dishes. Chopsticks are used for picking up the food – or in the case of soups, a broad, shallow spoon.

STEP 3

CHAPTER THIRTEEN

Seafood Dishes

As in the rest of China, Szechuan food features fish in many dishes, especially freshwater fish from the mighty Yangtze river, which flows through the region.

Szechuan dishes are noted for their hot, spicy character, and fish and seafood dishes are no exception. Whole fish, and fish fillets, are served in thick, spicy sauces, as in Braised Fish Fillets (see page 187). Shrimp dishes are equally hot and spicy, with garlic, ginger and chili appearing in almost every recipe – Szechuan Shrimp (see page 183) is a typical example.

Opposite: *The Yangtze river near Guilin. Until recently the Yangtze was Szechuan's main avenue of communication with the rest of China.*

STEP 2

STEP 3

STEP 3

STEP 4

SWEET & SOUR SHRIMP WITH WATER CHESTNUTS

*Use raw shrimp if possible. Omit steps 1 and 2 if
ready-cooked ones are used.*

SERVES 4

6–8 oz shelled raw jumbo or tiger shrimp
pinch salt
1 tsp egg white
1 tsp cornstarch paste (see page 231)
1¼ cups vegetable oil

SAUCE:
1 tbsp vegetable oil
½ small green bell pepper, cored, seeded and
    thinly sliced
½ small carrot, thinly sliced
4 oz canned water chestnuts, rinsed, drained
    and sliced
½ tsp salt
1 tbsp light soy sauce
2 tbsp sugar
3 tbsp rice or sherry vinegar
1 tsp Chinese rice wine or dry sherry
1 tbsp tomato sauce
½ tsp chili sauce
3–4 tbsp Chinese Stock (see page 230) or
    water
2 tsp cornstarch paste (see page 231)
a few drops sesame oil

1 Mix the shrimp with the salt, egg
white and cornstarch paste.

2 Heat the oil in a preheated wok and
stir-fry the shrimp for 30–40
seconds only. Remove and drain on
paper towels.

3 Pour off the oil and wipe the wok
clean with paper towels. To make
the sauce, first heat the tablespoon of oil.
Add the vegetables and stir-fry for about
1 minute, then add the seasonings with
the stock or water and bring to a boil.

4 Add the shrimp and stir until
blended well. Thicken the sauce
with the cornstarch paste and stir until
smooth. Sprinkle with sesame oil and
serve hot.

SESAME OIL

Sesame oil has a distinctive nutty flavor
and aroma. It is widely used in China as a
seasoning and is usually sprinkled on at
the last moment, to finish a dish. It is now
widely available in supermarkets. Use
sparingly.

SZECHUAN SHRIMP

Raw shrimp should be used if possible, otherwise omit steps 1 and 2 and add cooked shrimp before the sauce ingredients at the beginning of step 3.

SERVES 4

8–10 oz raw jumbo or tiger shrimp
pinch salt
½ egg white, lightly beaten
1 tsp cornstarch paste (see page 231)
2½ cups vegetable oil
fresh cilantro leaves, to garnish

SAUCE:
1 tsp finely chopped gingerroot
2 scallions, finely chopped
1 garlic clove, finely chopped
3–4 small dried red chilies, seeded and
   chopped
1 tbsp light soy sauce
1 tsp Chinese rice wine or dry sherry
1 tbsp tomato paste
1 tbsp oyster sauce
2–3 tbsp Chinese Stock (see page 230) or
   water
a few drops sesame oil

1 Peel the raw shrimp, then mix with the salt, egg white and cornstarch paste until well coated.

2 Heat the oil in a preheated wok until it is smoking. Deep-fry the shrimp in hot oil for about 1 minute. Remove with a slotted spoon and drain on paper towels.

3 Pour off the oil, leaving about 1 tablespoon in the wok. Add all the ingredients for the sauce, bring to a boil and stir until smooth and well blended.

4 Add the shrimp to the sauce and stir until blended well. Serve garnished with fresh cilantro leaves.

CHILIES

In Szechuan dishes chilies are often left unseeded, giving an extremely hot flavor to dishes. If you dislike very hot food, make sure the dried chilies are carefully seeded before use.

STEP 1

STEP 2

STEP 3

STEP 4

SZECHUAN STIR-FRIED SHRIMP

The bell peppers in this dish can be replaced by either snow peas or broccoli – the idea is to contrast the pinky/orange shrimp with a bright green vegetable.

SERVES 4

6 oz raw shrimp, shelled
1 tsp salt
¼ tsp egg white
2 tsp cornstarch paste (see page 231)
1¼ cups vegetable oil
1 scallion, cut into short sections
1-inch piece gingerroot, thinly sliced
1 small green bell pepper, cored, seeded
   and cubed
½ tsp sugar
1 tbsp light soy sauce
1 tsp Chinese rice wine or dry sherry
a few drops sesame oil

1 Mix the shrimp with a pinch of the salt, the egg white and cornstarch paste until they are all well coated.

2 Heat the oil in a preheated wok and stir-fry the shrimp for 30–40 seconds only. Remove and drain on paper towels.

3 Pour off the oil, leaving about 1 tablespoon in the wok. Add the scallion and ginger to flavor the oil for a few seconds, then add the green bell pepper and stir-fry for about 1 minute.

4 Add the remaining salt and the sugar followed by the shrimp. Continue stirring for another minute or so, then add the soy sauce and wine and blend well. Sprinkle with sesame oil and serve immediately.

COOK'S HINTS

One or 2 small green or red hot chilies, sliced, can be added with the green bell pepper to create a more spicy dish. Leave the chilies unseeded for a very hot dish.

Fresh gingerroot, sold by weight, should be peeled and sliced, then finely chopped or shredded before use. It will keep for weeks in a cool, dry place. Dried ginger powder is no substitute. In comparison with fresh gingerroot, it is lacking in flavor.

BRAISED FISH FILLETS

Any white fish such as lemon sole or flounder is ideal for this dish.

STEP 2

SERVES 4

3–4 small Chinese dried mushrooms
10–12 oz fish fillets
1 tsp salt
$^1\!/_2$ egg white, lightly beaten
1 tsp cornstarch paste (see page 231)
$2^1\!/_2$ cups vegetable oil
1 tsp finely chopped gingerroot
2 scallions, finely chopped
1 garlic clove, finely chopped
$^1\!/_2$ small green bell pepper, cored, seeded and
     cut into small cubes
$^1\!/_2$ small carrot, thinly sliced
2 oz canned sliced bamboo shoots, rinsed and
     drained
$^1\!/_2$ tsp sugar
1 tbsp light soy sauce
1 tsp Chinese rice wine or dry sherry
1 tbsp chili bean sauce
2–3 tbsp Chinese Stock (see page 230) or
     water
a few drops sesame oil

1 Soak the Chinese mushrooms in warm water for 30 minutes, then drain on paper towels, reserving the soaking water for stock or soup. Squeeze the mushrooms to extract all the moisture, cut off and discard any hard stems and slice thinly.

2 Cut the fish into bite-sized pieces, then place in a shallow dish and mix with a pinch of salt, the egg white and cornstarch paste, turning the fish to coat well.

STEP 3

3 Heat the oil and deep-fry the fish pieces for about 1 minute. Remove with a slotted spoon and drain on paper towels.

4 Pour off the oil, leaving about 1 tablespoon in the wok. Add the ginger, scallions and garlic to flavor the oil for a few seconds, then add the vegetables and stir-fry for about 1 minute.

STEP 4

5 Add the salt, sugar, soy sauce, wine, chili bean sauce and stock or water and bring to a boil. Add the fish pieces, stir to coat well with the sauce, and braise for another minute. Sprinkle with sesame oil and serve immediately.

STEP 5

STEP 1

STEP 2

STEP 3

STEP 3

FISH IN SZECHUAN HOT SAUCE

This is a classic Szechuan recipe. When served in a restaurant, the fish head and tail are removed before cooking.

SERVES 4

1 carp, bream, sea bass, trout, grouper or
   gray mullet, about 1¹/₂ lb, drawn
1 tbsp light soy sauce
1 tbsp Chinese rice wine or dry sherry
vegetable oil for deep-frying
flat-leaf parsley or cilantro sprigs, to garnish

SAUCE:
2 garlic cloves, finely chopped
2–3 scallions, finely chopped
1 tsp finely chopped gingerroot
2 tbsp chili bean sauce
1 tbsp tomato paste
2 tsp sugar
1 tbsp rice vinegar
¹/₂ cup Chinese Stock (see page 230) or
   water
1 tbsp cornstarch paste (see page 231)
¹/₂ tsp sesame oil

1 Wash the fish and dry well on paper towels. Score both sides of the fish to the bone with a sharp knife, making diagonal cuts at intervals about 1 inch apart. Rub the fish with the soy sauce and wine on both sides, then leave on a plate in the refrigerator to marinate for 10–15 minutes.

2 Heat the oil in a preheated wok until smoking. Deep-fry the fish in the hot oil for 3–4 minutes on both sides, or until golden brown.

3 Pour off the oil, leaving about 1 tablespoon in the wok. Push the fish to one side of the wok and add the garlic, white parts of the scallions, ginger, chili bean sauce, tomato paste, sugar, vinegar and stock. Bring to a boil and braise the fish in the sauce for 4–5 minutes, turning it over once.

4 Add the green parts of the scallions and stir in the cornstarch paste to thicken the sauce. Sprinkle with sesame oil and serve immediately, garnished with parsley or cilantro.

CHAPTER FOURTEEN

Meat & Poultry Dishes

Poultry is popular in Szechuan as elsewhere in China, though characteristically it is much hotter and spicier than elsewhere – Chili Chicken (see page 197) is a typical example.

Beef appears on the menu more often than in the South or East. A favorite form of cooking is stir-frying, giving a dry, chewy texture. Braising and steaming are also popular methods of cooking beef and pork, ensuring a tender result, and so too is double-cooking. This is a technique in which the meat is first tenderized by long, slow simmering in water, followed by a quick crisping or stir-frying in a sauce – Twice-cooked Pork (see page 203) is a delicious example of this technique.

Opposite: The fertile soil of Szechuan produces abundant crops almost all the year round.

STEP 1

STEP 2

STEP 2

STEP 4

AROMATIC & CRISPY DUCK

Although the pancakes traditionally served with this dish are not too difficult to make, the process is very time-consuming. Buy ready-made ones from Oriental stores, or use crisp lettuce leaves as the wrapper.

SERVES 4

2 large duckling quarters
1 tsp salt
3–4 pieces star anise
1 tsp Szechuan red peppercorns
1 tsp cloves
2 cinnamon sticks, broken into pieces
2–3 scallions, cut into short sections
4–5 small slices gingerroot
3–4 tbsp Chinese rice wine or dry sherry
vegetable oil for deep-frying

TO SERVE:
12 ready-made pancakes or 12 crisp lettuce
 leaves
hoi-sin or plum sauce
1/4 English cucumber, thinly shredded
3–4 scallions, thinly shredded

1 Rub the duck pieces with the salt and arrange the star anise, peppercorns, cloves and cinnamon on top. Sprinkle with the scallions, ginger and wine and let marinate for at least 3–4 hours.

2 Arrange the duck pieces (with the marinade spices) on a plate that will fit inside a bamboo steamer. Pour some hot water into a wok, place the bamboo steamer in the wok, sitting on a trivet. Put in the duck and cover with the bamboo lid. Steam the duck pieces (with the marinade) over high heat for at least 2–3 hours, until tender and cooked through. Top up the hot water from time to time as required.

3 Remove the duck and let cool for at least 4–5 hours – this is very important, for unless the duck is cold and dry, it will not be crispy.

4 Pour off the water and wipe the wok dry. Pour in the oil and heat until smoking. Deep-fry the duck pieces, skin-side down, for 4–5 minutes or until crisp and brown. Remove and drain on paper towels.

5 To serve, scrape the meat off the bone, place about 1 teaspoon of hoi-sin or plum sauce on the center of a pancake (or lettuce leaf), add a few pieces of cucumber and scallion with a portion of the duck meat. Wrap up to form a small parcel and eat with your fingers. Provide plenty of paper napkins for your guests.

STEP 1

STEP 2

STEP 3

STEP 4

KUNG PO CHICKEN WITH CASHEW NUTS

Peanuts, walnuts or almonds can be used instead of the cashew nuts, if preferred.

SERVES 4

8–10 oz boneless chicken meat, skinned
¼ tsp salt
⅓ egg white
1 tsp cornstarch paste (see page 231)
1 medium green bell pepper, cored and
  seeded
4 tbsp vegetable oil
1 scallion, cut into short sections
a few small gingerroot slices
4–5 small dried red chilies, soaked, seeded
  and shredded
2 tbsp crushed yellow bean sauce
1 tsp Chinese rice wine or dry sherry
1 cup roasted cashew nuts
a few drops sesame oil
boiled rice, to serve

1 Cut the chicken into small cubes about the size of bouillon cubes. Place the chicken in a small bowl and mix with a pinch of salt, the egg white and the cornstarch paste, in that order.

2 Cut the green bell pepper into cubes or triangles about the same size as the chicken pieces.

3 Heat the oil in a preheated wok. Add the chicken cubes and stir-fry for about 1 minute, or until the color

changes. Remove with a slotted spoon and keep warm.

4 Add the scallion, ginger, chilies and green bell pepper. Stir-fry for about 1 minute, then add the chicken with the yellow bean sauce and wine. Blend well and stir-fry for another minute. Finally stir in the cashew nuts and sesame oil. Serve hot.

VARIATIONS

Any nuts can be used in place of the cashew nuts, if preferred. The important point is the crunchy texture, which is very much a feature of Szechuan cooking.

SZECHUAN CHILI CHICKEN

*In China, the chicken pieces are chopped through the bone for this dish,
but if you do not possess a cleaver, use filleted chicken meat.*

STEP 1

SERVES 4

1 lb chicken thighs
¼ tsp pepper
1 tbsp sugar
2 tsp light soy sauce
1 tsp dark soy sauce
1 tbsp Chinese rice wine or dry sherry
2 tsp cornstarch
2–3 tbsp vegetable oil
1–2 garlic cloves, crushed
2 scallions, cut into short sections, with the
   green and white parts separated
4–6 small dried red chilies, soaked
   and seeded
2 tbsp crushed yellow bean sauce
about ⅔ cup Chinese Stock (see page 230)
   or water

1 Cut or chop the chicken thighs into
bite-sized pieces and marinate with
the pepper, sugar, soy sauce, wine and
cornstarch for 25–30 minutes.

2 Heat the oil in a preheated wok.
Add the chicken pieces and stir-fry
until lightly brown for about 1–2
minutes. Remove the chicken pieces with
a slotted spoon, transfer to a warm dish
and reserve.

3 Add the garlic, the white parts of
the scallions, the chilies and yellow
bean sauce to the wok and stir-fry for
about 30 seconds, blending well.

4 Return the chicken pieces to the
wok, stirring constantly for 1–2
minutes, then add the stock or water,
bring to a boil and cover. Braise over
medium heat for 5–6 minutes, stirring
once or twice. Garnish with the green
parts of the scallions and serve
immediately.

STEP 2

STEP 3

CHILIES

One of the striking features of Szechuan
cooking is the quantity of chilies used.
Food generally in this region is much
hotter than elsewhere in China – people
tend to keep a string of dry chilies hanging
from the eaves of their houses.

STEP 4

STEP 1

STEP 2

STEP 3

STEP 4

CHICKEN WITH BELL PEPPERS

Red bell pepper or celery can also be used in this recipe;
the method is the same.

SERVES 4

10 oz boned, skinned chicken breast
1 tsp salt
½ egg white
2 tsp cornstarch paste (see page 231)
1 medium green bell pepper, cored and
*   seeded*
1¼ cups vegetable oil
1 scallion, finely shredded
a few strips gingerroot, thinly
*   shredded*
1–2 red chilies, seeded and thinly shredded
½ tsp sugar
1 tbsp Chinese rice wine or dry sherry
a few drops sesame oil

1 Cut the chicken breast into strips,
then mix in a bowl with a pinch of
the salt, the egg white and cornstarch, in
that order.

2 Cut the green bell pepper into thin
shreds the same size and length as
the chicken strips.

3 Heat the oil in a preheated wok.
Add the chicken strips and deep-fry
them in batches for about 1 minute, or
until the color of the chicken changes.
Remove the chicken strips with a slotted

spoon and keep warm while you
complete the recipe.

4 Pour off the excess oil from the
wok, leaving about 1 tablespoon.
Add the scallion, ginger, chilies and
green bell pepper. Stir-fry for about 1
minute, then return the chicken to the
wok together with the remaining salt,
the sugar and wine. Stir-fry for another
minute, sprinkle with sesame oil and
serve.

RICE WINE

Rice wine is used everywhere in China for
both cooking and drinking. Made from
glutinous rice, it is known as "yellow
wine" (Huang jiu or chiew in Chinese)
because of its rich amber color. The best
variety is called Shao Hsing or Shaoxing,
and comes from the south-east of China.
Rice wine is more powerful than wines in
the West – about 16° proof – and sherry is
the best substitute as a cooking
ingredient.

STEP 1

STEP 1

STEP 3

STEP 4

FISH-FLAVORED SHREDDED PORK

"Fish-flavored" (yu-xiang in Chinese) is a Szechuan cookery term meaning that the dish is prepared with seasonings normally used in fish dishes.

SERVES 4

about 2 tbsp dried wood ears
8–10 oz pork tenderloin
1 tsp salt
2 tsp cornstarch paste (see page 231)
3 tbsp vegetable oil
1 garlic clove, finely chopped
1/2 tsp finely chopped gingerroot
2 scallions, finely chopped, with the white and green parts separated
2 celery stalks, thinly sliced
1/2 tsp sugar
1 tbsp light soy sauce
1 tbsp chili bean sauce
2 tsp rice vinegar
1 tsp Chinese rice wine or dry sherry
a few drops sesame oil

1 Soak the wood ears in warm water for about 20 minutes, then rinse in cold water until the water is clear. Drain well, then cut into thin shreds.

2 Cut the pork into thin shreds, then mix in a bowl with a pinch of salt and about half the cornstarch paste until well coated.

3 Heat 1 tablespoon of oil in a preheated wok. Add the pork strips and stir-fry for about 1 minute, or until the color changes, then remove with a slotted spoon.

4 Add the remaining oil to the wok and heat. Add the garlic, ginger, the white parts of the scallions, the wood ears and celery. Stir-fry for about 1 minute, then return the pork strips together with the salt, sugar, soy sauce, chili bean sauce, vinegar and wine. Blend well and continue stirring for another minute.

5 Finally add the green parts of the scallions and blend in the remaining cornstarch paste and sesame oil. Stir until the sauce has thickened and serve hot.

DRIED WOOD EARS

Also known as cloud ears, this is a dried gray-black fungus widely used in Szechuan cooking. It is always soaked in warm water before using. Wood ears have a crunchy texture and a mild flavor.

TWICE-COOKED PORK

Twice-cooked is a popular way of cooking meat in China. The meat is first boiled to tenderize it, then cut into strips or slices and stir-fried.

STEP 1

SERVES 4

8–10 oz shoulder or leg of pork, in one piece
1 small green bell pepper, cored and seeded
1 small red bell pepper, cored and seeded
4 oz canned sliced bamboo shoots, rinsed and
    drained
3 tbsp vegetable oil
1 scallion, cut into short sections
1 tsp salt
$\frac{1}{2}$ tsp sugar
1 tbsp light soy sauce
1 tsp chili bean sauce or very finely minced
    fresh chili
1 tsp Chinese rice wine or dry sherry
a few drops sesame oil

1 Immerse the pork in a pot of boiling water to cover. Return to a boil and skim the surface. Reduce the heat, cover and simmer for 15–20 minutes. Turn off the heat and let the pork cool in the water for 2–3 hours.

2 Remove the pork from the water and drain well. Trim off any excess fat, then cut into small, thin slices. Cut the green and red bell peppers into pieces about the same size as the pork and the sliced bamboo shoots.

3 Heat the oil in a preheated wok. Add the vegetables together with the scallion. Stir-fry for about 1 minute.

4 Add the pork, followed by the salt, sugar, soy sauce, chili bean sauce and wine. Blend well, continue stirring for another minute, then sprinkle with sesame oil and serve.

STEP 1

PREPARING THE MEAT

For ease of handling, buy a boned piece of meat, and roll into a compact shape. Tie securely with string before placing in the boiling water.

STEP 2

STEP 4

STEP 1

STEP 2

STEP 3

STEP 4

CRISPY SHREDDED BEEF

A very popular Szechuan dish served in most Chinese restaurants all over the world.

SERVES 4

10–12 oz beef steak, such as rump
   or sirloin
2 eggs
¼ tsp salt
4–5 tbsp all-purpose flour
vegetable oil for deep-frying
2 carrots, finely shredded
2 scallions, thinly shredded
1 garlic clove, finely chopped
2–3 small fresh green or red chilies, seeded
   and thinly shredded
4 tbsp sugar
3 tbsp rice vinegar
1 tbsp light soy sauce
2–3 tbsp Chinese Stock (see page 230) or
   water
1 tsp cornstarch paste (see page 231)

1 Cut the steak across the grain into thin strips. Beat the eggs in a bowl with the salt and flour, adding a little water if necessary. Add the beef strips and mix well until coated with the batter.

2 Heat the oil in a preheated wok until smoking. Add the beef strips and deep-fry for 4–5 minutes, stirring to separate the shreds. Remove with a slotted spoon and drain on paper towels.

3 Add the carrots to the wok and deep-fry for about 1–1½ minutes, then remove with a slotted spoon and drain on paper towels.

4 Pour off the excess oil, leaving about 1 tablespoon in the wok. Add the scallions, garlic, chilies and carrots and stir-fry for about 1 minute, then add the sugar, vinegar, soy sauce and stock or water, blend well and bring to a boil.

5 Stir in the cornstarch paste and simmer for a few minutes to thicken the sauce. Return the beef to the wok and stir until the shreds of meat are well coated with the sauce. Serve hot.

TEXTURES

This dish is typical of the chewy-textured food that is so popular in Szechuan. Unlike dishes in Eastern China many Szechuan dishes are fried with only the minimum of sauce to convey the seasonings: the sauce itself is not an important element in the dish as it is in Canton.

BEEF & CHILI BLACK BEAN SAUCE

It is not necessary to use the expensive cuts of beef steak for this recipe: the meat will be tender as it is cut into small thin slices and marinated.

STEP 1

STEP 2

STEP 3

STEP 4

Serves 4

8–10 oz beef steak, such as sirloin
1 small onion
1 small green bell pepper, cored and seeded
about 1¼ cups vegetable oil
1 scallion, cut into short sections
a few small gingerroot slices
1–2 small green or red chilies, seeded and sliced
2 tbsp crushed black bean sauce

MARINADE:
½ tsp baking soda or baking powder
½ tsp sugar
1 tbsp light soy sauce
2 tsp Chinese rice wine or dry sherry
2 tsp cornstarch paste (see page 231)
2 tsp sesame oil

1 Cut the beef into small thin strips. Mix together the marinade ingredients in a shallow dish, add the beef strips, turn to coat and let marinate for at least 2–3 hours – the longer the better.

2 Cut the onion and green bell pepper into small cubes.

3 Heat the oil in a preheated wok. Add the beef strips and stir-fry for about 1 minute, or until the color changes. Remove with a slotted spoon and drain on paper towels. Keep warm.

4 Pour off the excess oil, leaving about 1 tablespoon in the wok. Add the scallion, ginger, chilies, onion and green bell pepper and stir-fry for about 1 minute. Add the black bean sauce, stir until smooth then return the beef strips to the wok. Blend well and stir-fry for another minute. Serve hot.

MARINADES

Do make sure that you marinade the beef for the time specified – it will then be wonderfully soft and tender.

CHAPTER FIFTEEN

Vegetables, Rice & Noodles

With its fertile soil and warm humid climate, Szechuan is one of the most prosperous regions of China, and crops can be grown almost all year round. Fruit, vegetables and cereal crops grow in abundance, as well as mushrooms and fungi. Pickling, drying and salting techniques are used extensively to help preserve this abundance of food – partly because the humid climate makes it difficult to keep food fresh.

As with other dishes, these tend to be highly spiced, and are usually on the hot side. "Fish-flavored", as in the eggplant dish on page 215, sounds strange, but is a popular way of describing dishes cooked with a variety of spices and flavorings – it has nothing to do with fish, and tastes delicious!

Opposite: *Rice plants hanging up to dry on bamboo racks. Rice is a staple crop in China and the fertile soil of Szechuan produces vast quantities of it.*

STEP 1

STEP 2

STEP 3

STEP 4

MA-PO TOFU

Ma-Po was the wife of a Szechuan chef who created this popular dish in the middle of the 19th century. The beef can be replaced by Chinese dried mushrooms to make a vegetarian meal.

SERVES 4

3 cakes firm or extra firm tofu
3 tbsp vegetable oil
4 oz coarsely ground beef
$\frac{1}{2}$ tsp finely chopped garlic
1 leek, cut into short sections
$\frac{1}{2}$ tsp salt
1 tbsp black bean sauce
1 tbsp light soy sauce
1 tsp chili bean sauce
3–4 tbsp Chinese Stock (see page 230) or
    water
2 tsp cornstarch paste (see page 231)
a few drops sesame oil
black pepper
finely chopped scallions, to garnish

1 Cut the tofu into $\frac{1}{2}$-inch cubes, handling it carefully. Bring some water to a boil in a small pan or a wok, add the tofu and blanch for 2–3 minutes to harden. Remove and drain well.

2 Heat the oil in a preheated wok. Add the ground beef and garlic and stir-fry for about 1 minute, or until the color of the beef changes. Add the chopped leek, salt and sauces and continue stir-frying until all the ingredients are well blended.

3 Add the stock or water followed by the tofu. Bring to a boil and braise slowly for 2–3 minutes.

4 Add the cornstarch paste, and stir until the sauce has thickened. Sprinkle with sesame oil and black pepper and garnish with scallions. Serve hot.

TOFU

Tofu has been an important element in Chinese cooking for more than 1,000 years. It is made of yellow soy beans, which are soaked, ground and mixed with water. Tofu is highly nutritious, being rich in protein, and has a very bland taste. Solid cakes of tofu can be cut up with a sharp knife. Cook carefully as too much stirring can cause it to disintegrate.

STEP 1

STEP 1

STEP 3

STEP 4

BRAISED TOFU, HOME STYLE

The pork used in the recipe can be replaced by chicken or shrimp, or it can be omitted altogether.

SERVES 4

3 cakes tofu
4 oz boneless pork (or any other type
    of meat)
1 leek
1–2 scallions, cut into short sections
a few small dried whole chilies, soaked
vegetable oil for deep-frying
2 tbsp crushed yellow bean sauce
1 tbsp light soy sauce
2 tsp Chinese rice wine or dry sherry
a few drops sesame oil

1 Split each tofu cake into 3 slices crosswise, then cut each slice diagonally into 2 triangles.

2 Cut the pork into small thin slices or shreds; cut the leek into thin strips. Drain the chilies, remove the seeds using the tip of a knife, then cut into small shreds.

3 Heat the oil in a preheated wok until smoking. Deep-fry the tofu triangles for 2–3 minutes or until golden brown all over. Remove with a slotted spoon and drain on paper towels.

4 Pour off the hot oil, leaving about 1 tablespoon in the wok. Add the pork strips, scallions and chilies and stir-fry for about 1 minute or until the pork changes color.

5 Add the leek, tofu, yellow bean sauce, soy sauce and wine and braise for 2–3 minutes, stirring very gently to blend everything well. Finally sprinkle on the sesame oil and serve.

BRAISED TOFU

Tofu is sold in 4 forms: extra firm, firm, soft or extra soft, known as silken tofu. It is the extra firm or firm kinds that are used for braising and stir-frying. Silken tofu is usually added to soups or sauces. It is also possible to buy dried tofu and smoked tofu in specialist Oriental stores. It is acceptable to store tofu for a few days if it is submerged in water in an air-tight container, then placed in the refrigerator.

FISH EGGPLANT

Like Fish-flavored Shredded Pork (see page 200), there is no fish involved in this dish, and the meat can be omitted without affecting the flavor.

STEP 1

SERVES 4

1 lb eggplant
vegetable oil for deep-frying
1 garlic clove, finely chopped
$\frac{1}{2}$ tsp finely chopped gingerroot
2 scallions, finely chopped, with the white and green parts separated
4 oz pork tenderloin, thinly shredded (optional)
1 tbsp light soy sauce
2 tsp Chinese rice wine or dry sherry
1 tbsp chili bean sauce
$\frac{1}{2}$ tsp salt
$\frac{1}{2}$ tsp sugar
1 tbsp rice vinegar
2 tsp cornstarch paste (see page 231)
a few drops sesame oil

1 Cut the eggplant into rounds and then into thin strips about the size of French fries – the skin can be peeled or left on.

2 Heat the oil in a preheated wok until smoking. Add the eggplant fries and deep-fry for 3–4 minutes, or until soft. Remove and drain on paper towels.

3 Pour off the hot oil, leaving about 1 tablespoon in the wok. Add the

garlic, ginger and the white parts of the scallions, followed by the pork (if using). Stir-fry for about 1 minute or until the color of the meat changes, then add the soy sauce, wine and chili bean sauce, blending them in well.

4 Return the eggplant fries to the wok together with the salt, sugar and vinegar. Continue stirring for another minute or so, then add the cornstarch paste and stir until the sauce has thickened.

5 Add the green parts of the scallions to the wok and sprinkle on the sesame oil. Serve hot.

FISH-FLAVORED DISHES

These multiple-flavored dishes, using garlic, chili sauce, vinegar, sugar and soy sauce all together, are always described as "fish-flavored", although there is no fish in the recipe. These dishes are only found in Szechuan.

STEP 2

STEP 3

STEP 4

STEP 1

STEP 2

STEP 3

STEP 4

STIR-FRIED SEASONAL VEGETABLES

When selecting different fresh vegetables for this dish, bear in mind that there should always be a contrast in color as well as texture.

SERVES 4

1 medium red bell pepper, cored and seeded
4 oz zucchini
4 oz cauliflower
4 oz green beans
3 tbsp vegetable oil
a few small gingerroot slices
$^1\!/_2$ tsp salt
$^1\!/_2$ tsp sugar
Chinese Stock (see page 230) or water
1 tbsp light soy sauce
a few drops sesame oil (optional)

1 Cut the red bell pepper into small squares. Thinly slice the zucchini. Trim the cauliflower and divide into small flowerets, discarding any thick stems. Make sure the vegetables are cut into roughly similar shapes and sizes to ensure even cooking.

2 Top and tail the green beans, then cut them in half.

3 Heat the oil in a pre-heated wok. Add the vegetables and stir-fry with the ginger for about 2 minutes.

4 Add the salt and sugar to the wok, and continue to stir-fry for 1–2 minutes, adding a little Chinese stock or water if the vegetables appear to be too dry. Do not add liquid unless it seems necessary.

5 Add the light soy sauce and sesame oil (if using), blend well to lightly coat the vegetables and serve at once.

VEGETABLES

Almost any vegetables could be used in this dish: other good choices would be snow peas, broccoli flowerets, carrots, baby corn cobs, green peas, Chinese leaves and young spinach leaves. Either white or black (oyster) mushrooms can also be used to give a greater diversity of textures. Make sure there is a good variety of color, and always include several crisp vegetables such as carrots or snow peas.

STEP 1

STEP 2

STEP 3

STEP 4

BRAISED CHINESE LEAVES

White cabbage can be used instead of the Chinese leaves for this dish.

SERVES 4

1 lb Chinese leaves or white cabbage
3 tbsp vegetable oil
$^1/_2$ tsp Szechuan red peppercorns
5–6 small dried red chilies, seeded and
    minced
$^1/_2$ tsp salt
1 tbsp sugar
1 tbsp light soy sauce
1 tbsp rice vinegar
a few drops sesame oil (optional)

1 Shred the Chinese leaves or cabbage crosswise into thin pieces. (If Chinese leaves are unavailable, the best alternative to use in this recipe is a firm-packed white cabbage; not the dark green type of cabbage. Cut out the thick core of the cabbage with a sharp knife before shredding.)

2 Heat the oil in a pre-heated wok. Add the Szechuan red peppercorns and dried red chilies and stir for a few seconds.

3 Add the Chinese leaves or shredded cabbage to the peppercorns and chilies, stir-fry for about 1 minute, then add salt and continue stirring for another minute.

4 Add the sugar, soy sauce and vinegar, blend well and braise for 1 more minute. Finally sprinkle on the sesame oil, if using. Serve hot or cold.

PEPPERCORNS

It is important to use the correct type of peppercorns in preparing this dish. Szechuan red peppercorns are also known as farchiew. They are not true peppers, but reddish brown dry berries with a pungent, aromatic odor which distinguishes them from the hotter black peppercorns. Roast them briefly in the oven or sauté them in a dry skillet. Grind the peppercorns in a blender and store in a jar until needed.

STEP 1

STEP 2

STEP 3

STEP 4

CHICKEN OR PORK CHOW MEIN

*This is a basic recipe – the meat and/or vegetables can be
varied as much as you like.*

SERVES 4

8 oz Chinese egg noodles
4–5 tbsp vegetable oil
4 oz green beans
8 oz chicken breast meat, or pork tenderloin,
   cooked
2 tbsp light soy sauce
1 tsp salt
$\frac{1}{2}$ tsp sugar
1 tbsp Chinese rice wine or dry sherry
2 scallions, finely shredded
a few drops sesame oil
chili sauce, to serve (optional)

1 Cook the noodles in boiling water according to the instructions on the package, then drain and rinse under cold water. Drain again and toss with 1 tablespoon of the oil.

2 Slice the meat into thin shreds and top and tail the beans.

3 Heat 3 tablespoons of oil in a preheated wok until hot. Add the noodles and stir-fry for 2–3 minutes with 1 tablespoon soy sauce, then remove to a serving dish. Keep warm.

4 Heat the remaining oil and stir-fry the beans and meat for

about 2 minutes. Add the salt, sugar, wine, the remaining soy sauce and about half the scallions to the wok.

5 Blend the meat mixture well and add a little stock if necessary, then pour on top of the noodles, and sprinkle with sesame oil and the remaining scallions. Serve hot or cold with or without chili sauce.

CHOW MEIN

Chow Mein literally means "stir-fried noodles" and is highly popular in the West as well as in China. Almost any ingredient can be added, such as fish, meat, poultry or vegetables. It is very popular for lunch and makes a tasty salad served cold.

STEP 2

STEP 3

STEP 4

STEP 5

NOODLES IN SOUP

Noodles in soup (tang mein) are far more popular than fried noodles (chow mein) in China. You can use different ingredients for the dressing according to taste.

SERVES 4

8 oz chicken meat, pork tenderloin, or any
    other ready-cooked meat
3–4 Chinese dried mushrooms, soaked
4 oz canned sliced bamboo shoots, rinsed and
    drained
1 1/2 cups spinach leaves, lettuce hearts or
    Chinese leaves, shredded
2 scallions, finely shredded
8 oz egg thread noodles
about 2 1/2 cups Chinese Stock (see page
    230)
2 tbsp light soy sauce
2 tbsp vegetable oil
1 tsp salt
1/2 tsp sugar
2 tsp Chinese rice wine or dry sherry
a few drops sesame oil
1 tsp red chili oil (optional)

1 Cut the meat into thin shreds.
Squeeze dry the soaked mushrooms
and discard the hard stems.

2 Thinly shred the mushrooms,
bamboo shoots, spinach leaves
and scallions.

3 Cook the noodles in boiling water
according to the instructions on the
package, then drain and rinse under cold
water. Place in a bowl. Bring the stock to
a boil, add about 1 tablespoon soy sauce
and pour over the noodles. Keep warm.

4 Heat the oil in a pre-heated wok.
Add about half of the scallions, the
meat and the vegetables (mushrooms,
bamboo shoots and greens). Stir-fry for
2–3 minutes. Add all the seasonings and
blend well.

5 Pour the mixture in the wok over
the noodles, garnish with the
remaining scallions and serve
immediately.

NOODLE SOUP

Noodle soup is wonderfully satisfying and
is ideal to serve on cold winter days.

EGG FRIED RICE

*The rice used for frying should not be too soft. Ideally, the rice should
have been slightly undercooked and left to cool before frying.*

SERVES 4

3 eggs
1 tsp salt
2 scallions, finely chopped
2–3 tbsp vegetable oil
3 cups cooked rice, well drained and cooled
   (see note in step 3)
1 cup cooked peas

1 Lightly beat the eggs with a pinch
of salt and 1 tablespoon of the
scallions.

2 Heat the oil in a preheated wok.
Add the eggs and stir until lightly
scrambled. (The eggs should only be
cooked until they start to set, so they are
still moist.)

3 Add the rice and stir to make sure
that each grain of rice is separated.
Note: the cooked rice should be cool,
preferably cold, so that much of the
moisture has evaporated. This ensures
that the oil will coat the grains of rice and
prevent them sticking. Store the cooked
rice in the refrigerator until ready to
cook. Make sure the oil is really hot
before adding the rice, to avoid the rice
being saturated with oil otherwise it will
be heavy and greasy.

4 Add the remaining salt, scallions
and peas. Blend well and serve hot
or cold.

PERFECT FRIED RICE

Use rice with a fairly firm texture. Ideally,
the raw rice should be soaked in water for
a short time before cooking. The two main
varieties of rice available are long-grain
and short-grain. While it used to be
necessary to wash rice, processing now
makes this unnecessary. Short-grain
Oriental rice can be substituted for long-
grain.

Fried rice lends itself to many
variations. You may choose to add other
vegetables as well as the scallions, if
desired, as well as shrimp, ham or
chicken.

The Chinese Diet

THE CHINESE DIET

SPECIAL INGREDIENTS

Here are a few of the ingredients commonly used in Chinese cooking. They are becoming widely available, particularly in larger supermarkets and health-food stores, but substitutes can be used for the more unusual items.

Black beans
Salted fermented soy beans, available in packages or cans.

Chilies
These can be red or green, and come in a variety of sizes – the smaller the chili, the hotter it is, and dried chilies are hotter than fresh. Take care when handling them, as chili juice stings; avoid touching your eyes and always wash your hands thoroughly afterwards. Discard the seeds, as these are the hottest part.

Chili oil
A very hot oil flavored by chilies and red in color; use sparingly. You can make your own by adding a few dried chilies to some oil and leaving them to soak for a few days to allow the flavor to come out.

China can be divided into four main regions of cuisine, all of which share a wealth of foodstuffs and a diversity of cookery styles. The variety of Chinese cooking appeals to people in every corner of the globe, not only because of the range of unusual and exotic ingredients but because the daily diet is based largely on vegetables, rice and fresh noodles. Fish and meat are normally added for flavor, and dairy products are not used. The Chinese diet is considered to be one of the healthiest in the world.

The art of Chinese cooking is thought to be particularly ancient. Tea was known as a drink in China as long as 2,000 years ago. And even today, the Taoist philosophy of Yin and Yang is still generally practised, so that balance and contrast underlies all Chinese cookery and thus distinguishes it from any other food culture.

To enjoy the book to the full, take advantage of these Special Techniques pages before proceeding with the recipes and you will soon appreciate the speed and ease with which Chinese food can be cooked, whether it is for a complete meal or simply as an accompaniment to your normal food.

An overview
China is a vast country situated in a dominant position in the eastern part of Asia – in size it is equivalent to Western Europe. Even though it lies mainly within the temperate zone both geographically and climatically, the regions are widely diverse. From the Tibetan Plateau in the west (12,000 ft), the country descends continually eastwards until it arrives at the Yangtze flood plain. It is the diversity of the countryside that has given rise to the wide variety of produce and the great range of regional cooking styles. China breaks down into four distinct regions, each of which has its own style of cuisine and specialities.

Cantonese (Southern School)
The best-known cuisine in the western world because of the large numbers of Chinese that emigrated from Canton to Europe and America in the nineteenth century. Also, because Canton was the first Chinese port opened for trade, it is the most influenced by foreign contact and offers the widest variety of food. Light and subtle flavorings are used and the food is less fatty than in other regions. It is famous for its seafood specialties as well as its sweet and sour dishes and crispy pork recipes.

Shanghai (Eastern School)
This region is rich in fruit and vegetables, and is well known for its vegetarian cuisine as well as its fresh fish. Sugar and oil are used in large quantities, earning the area a reputation for rich food.

Szechuan (Western School)
The Szechuan cuisine is characterized by its dependence on strong flavorings and hot spices such as red chilies, Szechuan peppercorns, ginger and garlic.

Peking (Northern School)
The staple food is mainly wheat, corn and maize, rather than rice, with an emphasis on noodles, dumplings and pancakes. Due to the harsh winter, many food products are preserved by drying, smoking or pickling.

The principles of Chinese cooking
What distinguishes Chinese cooking from all other food cultures is the emphasis on the harmonious blending of color, aroma, flavor and texture, both in a single dish and in a course of dishes for a meal. Balance and contrast are the key words. Chinese cooks from the housewife to the professional chef all work to this yin–yang principle: harmonious balance and contrast by varying the ingredients, cutting shapes, seasonings and cooking methods.

In order to achieve this, two most important factors should be observed, that is, heat and timing – the degree of heat and duration of cooking, which means the right cooking method for the right food. This is why the size and shape of the cut ingredient must, first of all, be suitable for a particular method of cooking. For instance, ingredients for quick stir-frying should be cut into small, thin slices or shreds of uniform size, never into large, thick chunks. This is not just for the sake of appearance, but also because ingredients of the same size and shape require about the same amount of cooking time.

Bear these general points in mind when you cook Chinese food and you will find it surprisingly easy to create delicious dishes that are also a visual delight.

A healthy option
The daily diet of the Chinese is one of the healthiest in the world. Being such a vast country, China encompasses a number of different climates, which gives rise to a wide variety of produce. In addition, the selection of vegetables available in the markets has increased in recent years as China's peasants have been encouraged to grow their own crops.

The vegetarian element
Widespread poverty means that many people are unable to afford meat. Also, many follow a vegetarian diet for religious reasons. But even when they have the choice, the Chinese have many reasons for eating more vegetarian food than other kinds. They recognize that a largely vegetarian diet, based on vegetables and carbohydrates (such as rice or noodles) with only a little fish or meat, is the healthiest way to eat, In addition, it is more economical to use the land for growing vegetables and rice than for grazing livestock, as the crops will feed far more people than the livestock will.

EATING THE CHINESE WAY

Chinese cooking is one of the oldest known cuisines, and its influence has spread throughout the world. Its essence is harmony of flavor, color and texture. The recipes in this book have been designed to achieve exactly this. They are quick and simple to prepare and they mostly use ingredients obtainable from supermarkets. Occasionally, you may need to visit a Chinese food store to find one or two ingredients. Some of the

Lemongrass
An aromatic herb, available as fresh stems or dried as powder. Chop or slice the lower part of the stem to use.

Lily flowers
Also known as golden needles, these are dried lily-flower buds. Soak in water before use.

Lotus leaves
Leaves of the lotus plant. They are very large and sold dried. Soak in hot water before use. These are often used as a shell in which other ingredients are cooked, such as steamed rice.

Noodles
Made from rice, pulses or wheat. There is a large variety available, all of which can be interchanged in recipes. Cook according to package instructions as times vary from one type to another.

Sesame seeds
Add texture and a nutty flavor. Dry-fry to add color and accentuate the flavor.

CHINESE STOCK

This basic stock is used not only as the basis for soup-making, but also for general use in Chinese cooking.

MAKES 10 CUPS

1¹/₂ lb chicken pieces
1¹/₂ lb pork spareribs
15 cups cold water
3–4 pieces gingerroot, crushed
3–4 scallions each tied into a knot
3–4 tbsp Chinese rice wine or dry sherry

1. Trim off excess fat from the chicken and spareribs; chop them into large pieces.

2. Place the chicken and pork in a large pan with water; add the ginger and scallion knots.

3. Bring to a boil, and skim off the scum. Reduce heat and simmer uncovered for at least 2–3 hours.

4. Strain the stock, discarding the chicken, pork, ginger and scallions; add the wine and return to a boil, simmer for 2–3 minutes.

Refrigerate the stock. When cool, it will keep for up to 4–5 days. Alternatively, it can be frozen in small containers and be defrosted as required.

recipes have been adapted for the vegetarian from traditional Chinese recipes, and others are vegetarian dishes that have been developed to suit the Western kitchen.

Meal times in China are often family gatherings, at which many different dishes are served. A wide range of ingredients is used, but the different flavors of the many dishes are always made to work together. The meal is served all at once, including the soup. Unlike the Western convention, the Chinese never serve an individual dish to each person; all the dishes on the table are shared.

Preparing a Chinese meal

When planning a menu for this kind of shared meal, allow one dish per person. For example, if you are cooking for only two or three people, serve one main dish with one vegetable side dish and one rice or noodle dish, plus a soup if desired. For an informal meal for four to six people, serve four dishes plus soup and rice; for a formal dinner for approximately the same number of people, allow a range of six to eight dishes. Always increase the number of dishes rather than the quantity of ingredients when cooking for many people, as this will give more variety and contrast of taste, color and flavor on the table.

Do not choose too many dishes that need a lot of last-minute preparation or have to be served immediately, such as stir-fries. Vary the dishes so that some may be prepared in advance, and then you too can enjoy the meal and not spend all evening in the kitchen.

GLOSSARY OF INGREDIENTS

The list covers the most commonly used ingredients in Chinese cooking. These ingredients are becoming much more widely available, particularly in the supermarkets, health food shops and Chinese stores. Substitutes can often be used for the more unusual ingredients.

Baby corn Baby corn cobs have a wonderfully sweet fragrance and flavor, and irresistible texture. They are available both fresh and canned.

Bamboo shoots Available in cans only. Once opened, the contents may be kept in fresh water in a covered jar in the refrigerator for up to a week.

Bean sprouts Fresh bean sprouts, from mung or soy beans, are widely available from Oriental stores and supermarkets. They can be kept in the refrigerator for two to three days.

Bean sauce Available in black or yellow, bean sauce is made from crushed salted soy beans mixed with flour and spices (such as ginger or chili) to make a thickish paste. It is used for flavoring dishes or as a condiment. The sauce is sold in cans or jars and once opened should be stored in the refrigerator.

Chili bean sauce Fermented bean paste mixed with hot chilies and other seasonings. Sold in jars, some sauces are quite mild, but others are very hot. You will have to try out the various brands to see which one is to your taste.

Chinese leaves Also known as Chinese cabbage, there are two widely available varieties to be found in supermarkets and greengrocers. The most commonly seen one is a pale green color and has a tightly wrapped, elongated head – about two-thirds of the cabbage is stem, which has a crunchy texture. The other variety has a shorter, fatter head with curlier, pale yellow or green leaves, also with white stems.

Dried Chinese mushrooms (shiitake) Highly fragrant dried mushrooms which add a special flavor to Chinese dishes. There are many different varieties, but shiitake are the best. They are not cheap, but a small amount will go a long way, and they will keep indefinitely in an air-tight jar. Soak them in warm water for 20–30 minutes (or in cold water for several hours), squeeze dry and discard the hard stems before use.

Cilantro Fresh cilantro leaves, also known as Chinese parsley or coriander, have a distinctive flavor. Cilantro is widely used in Chinese cooking. It can be chopped and added to sauces and stuffing. The feathery leaves make an attractive garnish. Parsley can be used as a substitute.

Egg noodles There are many varieties of noodles in China, ranging from flat, broad ribbons to long, narrow strands. Both dried and fresh noodles are readily available.

Five-spice powder A mixture of star anise, fennel seeds, cloves, cinnamon bark and Szechuan pepper. It is very pungent so should be used sparingly. It will keep in an airtight container indefinitely.

Garlic A primary seasoning in Chinese food that not only adds flavor but has health-giving properties. Garlic may be chopped, crushed or pickled and is very often used in sauces and stuffings. Store garlic in a cool, dry area, not in the fridge where it will go moldy.

Gingerroot Fresh gingerroot, sold by the weight, should be peeled and then sliced, finely chopped or shredded before use. It will keep for several weeks in a dry, cool place. Dried ginger powder is no substitute.

Oils The most commonly used oil in Chinese cooking is peanut oil, which, because of its light flavor, is especially good in stir-frying and deep frying. Rape or sunflower oils are also popular, while butter is never used, and lard and chicken fat only occasionally.

Oyster sauce A thickish soy-based sauce used as a flavoring in Cantonese cooking. Sold in bottles, it will keep in the refrigerator for months.

Plum sauce Plum sauce has a unique, fruity flavor – a sweet and sour sauce with a difference.

Rice vinegar There are two basic types of rice vinegar. Red vinegar is made from fermented rice and has a distinctive dark color and depth of flavor. White vinegar

CORNSTARCH PASTE

Cornstarch paste is made by mixing 1 part cornstarch with about 1.5 parts of cold water. Stir until smooth. Use to thicken sauces.

SHRIMP WITH DIP SAUCE

10 oz raw shrimp, defrosted if frozen
1 tsp salt
4 cups water
2 scallions, shredded
2–3 slices gingerroot, shredded
2 green or red chilies, seeded and finely shredded
1 tbsp light soy sauce
1 tbsp red rice vinegar
1 tsp sesame seed oil

1. Poach the shrimp in boiling, salted water for 1 minute, then turn off the heat. Let stand for 1 minute, remove with a slotted spoon and drain on paper towels.

2. Place the scallions, ginger and chilies in a small heatproof bowl. Heat the oil and pour into the bowl. Add the soy sauce, vinegar and sesame oil and stir well.

3. Shell the shrimp, leaving the tails, and arrange on a serving dish. Serve with the dip sauce.

PLAIN RICE

Use long-grain or patna rice, or better still, try fragrant Thai rice.

SERVES 4

1¼ cups long-grain rice
about 1 cup cold water
pinch of salt
½ tsp oil (optional)

1. Wash and rinse the rice just once. Place the rice in a saucepan and add enough water so that there is no more than ½ inch of water above the surface of the rice.

2. Bring to a boil, add salt and oil (if using), and stir to prevent the rice sticking to the bottom of the pan.

3. Reduce the heat to very, very low. Cover and cook for 15–20 minutes.

4. Remove from the heat and let stand, covered, for 10 minutes or so. Fluff up the rice with a fork or spoon before serving.

is stronger in flavor as it is distilled from rice wine.

Rice wine Chinese rice wine, made from glutinous rice, is also known as "Yellow wine" (*Huang jiu* or *chiew* in Chinese), because of its golden color. The best variety, from south-east China, is called Shao Hsing or Shaoxing. A good dry or medium sherry can be an acceptable substitute.

Sesame oil Aromatic oil sold in bottles and widely used as a finishing touch, added to dishes just before serving. The refined yellow sesame oil sold in Middle Eastern stores is not so aromatic, has less flavor and therefore is not a very satisfactory substitute.

Sherry If rice wine is difficult to obtain, a good quality, dry pale sherry can be used instead. Cream or sweet sherry should not be substituted.

Soy sauce Sold in bottles or cans, this popular Chinese sauce is used both for cooking and at the table. Light soy sauce has more flavor than the sweeter, dark soy sauce, which gives the food a rich, reddish color.

Straw mushrooms Grown on beds of rice straw, hence the name, straw mushrooms have a pleasant slippery texture, and a subtle taste. Canned straw mushrooms should be rinsed and drained after opening.

Szechuan peppercorns Also known as *farchiew*, these are wild reddish-brown peppercorns from Szechuan. More aromatic but less hot than either white or black peppercorns, they do give a unique and delicious flavor to a variety of dishes.

Szechuan preserved vegetable This is a specialty of Szechuan province. It is the root of a special variety of the mustard green pickled in salt and hot chili. Sold in cans, once opened it can be stored in a sealed jar in the refrigerator for months.

Tofu This custard-like preparation of liquidized and pressed yellow soy beans is exceptionally high in protein. Tofu has a distinctive texture but a bland flavor. It is usually sold in two forms: in cakes about 3-inch square and 1-inch thick or as a semi-thick jelly. There is also a dried form, which is sold in Oriental and health-food stores. For solid tofu, use a sharp knife to cut the required amount into cubes or shreds. Cook carefully as it will break up if stirred too much. Tofu will keep for a few days if put in a container, submerged in water and placed in a refrigerator.

Water chestnuts The roots of the plant *Heleocharis tuberosa*. Also known as horse's hooves in China on account of their appearance before the skin is peeled off. They are available fresh or in cans. Canned water chestnuts retain only part of the texture, and even less of the flavor, of fresh ones. Will keep for about a month in the refrigerator in a covered jar, changing the water every two or three days.

Wood ears Also known as cloud ears, this is a dried black fungus. Sold in plastic bags in Oriental stores, it should be soaked in cold or warm water for 20 minutes, then rinsed in fresh water before use. It has a crunchy texture and mild but subtle flavor. Fresh "Jews ears" are a good substitute.

Wonton skins or wrappers These are made from flour, egg and water. They can be deep fried and served with a dipping sauce, or filled prior to deep frying, steaming or boiling. Buy them ready-made or make your own. Layers of filo pastry make a reasonable substitute. They can be kept frozen for up to six months.

ADDED EXTRAS

In addition to the staple ingredients shown in this section, there are delicious Chinese sauces you can add while cooking your dish, or just before serving it, which will enhance its authentic flavor. Here are a couple of suggestions:

Hoi-sin sauce Also known as barbecue sauce, this is made from soy beans, sugar, flour, vinegar, salt, garlic, chili and sesame seed oil. Sold in cans or jars, it will keep in the refrigerator for several months.

Chili sauce Very hot sauce made from chilies, vinegar, sugar and salt. Usually sold in bottles and should be used sparingly in cooking or as a dip. Tabasco sauce can be a substitute if you do not happen to have the real thing.

GARNISHES

Chinese food should always be pleasing to the eye as well as the palate. The dishes can be intricately decorated with delicately cut vegetables, adding color as well as a finishing touch. The garnishes can be as simple or elaborate as you wish, depending on time and patience. The more simple garnishes could be sprigs of fresh or chopped herbs such as cilantro, chervil or chives, shreds of scallion, chili, lemon zest or radish, or twists of lime or lemon. Some more elaborate garnishes are described below. Experiment with both for the best results.

Cucumber fans Cut a 3-inch long piece of English cucumber and divide this in half lengthwise. Lay a piece of cucumber cut side down and, using a small, sharp knife, cut thin slices along the length to within ½ inch of the end. Carefully turn alternate slices over in half and tuck in. Place in iced water until required.

Carrot flowers Peel the carrot. Using a sharp knife, make about five or six tiny V-shaped cuts along the length. Then cut into slices: the V-shapes will ensure each slice looks like a flower petal.

Fresh chili flowers Trim the tip of the chili but do not remove the skin. Make four cuts lengthwise from the stem of the chili to the tip to make four sections. Remove and discard any seeds. Soak the chilies in cold water – they will then flower in the water.

CHINESE FRUIT SALAD

The Chinese do not usually have desserts to finish off a meal, except at banquets and special occasions. Sweet dishes are usually served in between main meals as snacks, but fruit is refreshing at the end of a big meal.

1 cup rock candy or crystal sugar
2½ cups boiling water
1 large honeydew melon
4–5 different fruits, such as
pineapple, grapes, banana,
mango, lychees or kiwi fruit

1. Dissolve the rock candy in the boiling water, then let cool.

2. Slice 1 inch off the top of the melon and scoop out the flesh, discarding the seeds. Cut the flesh into small chunks. Prepare the other fruits and cut into small chunks.

3. Fill the melon shell with the fruits and the syrup. Cover with plastic wrap and chill for at least 2 hours. Serve on a bed of crushed ice.

EXTRA GARNISHES

Shrimp crackers These consist of compressed slivers of shrimp and flour paste. They expand into large, translucent crisps when deep fried.

Radish flowers Trim each end of the radish. Using a sharp knife, make "V" cuts around the top and remove the cut parts to expose the whites of the radish.

Radish roses For radish roses, trim the ends, then hold the knife flat to the radish skin and make short vertical cuts around the sides, as if you were shaving off the outer skin, but without detaching each "petal". Plunge straight into iced water.

Tomato roses For tomato roses, peel off the skin of a tomato using a sharp knife in one long strip. Curl the skin into a circle.

EQUIPMENT

There are only a few basic implements in the Chinese *batterie de cuisine* that are considered essential in order to achieve the best results. Equivalent equipment is available in a Western kitchen, but Chinese utensils are of an ancient design, usually made of inexpensive materials, have been in continuous use for thousands of years and do serve a special function. Their more sophisticated and expensive Western counterparts prove rather inadequate in contrast.

Chinese cleaver Good, strong, sharp kitchen knives are more than adequate but it is worth trying to work with a Chinese cleaver. The wide blade looks clumsy, but the corner of the blade can do anything the point of a knife can do. A cleaver is the best thing for slicing, shredding, chopping and dicing, and, the wide blade can carry chopped ingredients from the board to the cooking pot.

Cleavers vary in weight and thickness of blade; the heavier type, for chopping through bones, is used a lot in Chinese cooking, while the lighter, sharper type is ideal for delicate, precision work. It is best to work with the cleaver on a wooden board as the surface is not slippery and is therefore safer to use.

Chopping block The Chinese traditionally worked on a chopping block – a cross-section of a tree-trunk about 16 inches across and 6 inches thick. Sturdy and porous, it is, however, difficult to obtain.

Wok The round-bottomed iron wok conducts and retains heat evenly, and because of its shape, the ingredients always return to the center, where the heat is most intense, however vigorously you stir. The wok is also ideal for deep frying – its conical shape requires far less oil than the flat-bottomed deep fryer, and has more depth (which means more heat) and more cooking surface (which means more food can be cooked at one go). Besides being a skillet, a wok is also used for braising, steaming, boiling and poaching etc. – in other words, the whole spectrum of Chinese cooking methods can be executed in one single utensil.

It is essential that a new iron wok is seasoned properly before use. Prepare it by washing thoroughly in hot water and detergent then drying it well. To season, put it over a gentle heat and, when the metal heats up, wipe over the entire inner surface with a pad of paper towels that you have first dipped in oil. Repeat with fresh oiled paper until the paper stays clean. Your wok is then ready to use.

Steamers Steaming can be done in any covered pot large enough to take a plate which is placed on a rack to hold it above the boiling water. There has to be space for the steam to circulate. The food is put on the plate and a well-fitting lid put on top. A wok with its own lid will serve very well. The traditional Chinese steamer is made of bamboo and is particularly well-adapted to steaming as the gaps in the bamboo allow excess steam to escape; the modern version is made of aluminium.

Frying spoons These spoons of fine wire mesh are useful for lifting small pieces of food out of the oil, as is a large wire spoon that can lift an entire fish out.

Ladle and spatula Wok sets usually consist of a pair of stirrers in the form of a ladle and spatula. Of the two, the flat ladle or scooper (as it is sometimes called) is more versatile. It is used by the Chinese cook for adding ingredients and seasonings to the wok, besides being a stirring implement.

Strainers There are two basic types of strainers – one is made of copper or steel wire with long bamboo handles, the other of perforated metal (iron or stainless steel). Several different sizes are available.

Chopsticks Does Chinese food taste any better when eaten with chopsticks? This is not merely an aesthetic question, but also a practical point, partly because all Chinese food is prepared in such a way that it is easily picked up by chopsticks.

Learning to use chopsticks is quite easy – simply place one chopstick in the hollow between thumb and index finger and rest its lower end below the first joint of the third finger. This chopstick remains stationary. Hold the other chopstick between the tips of the the index and middle finger, steady its upper half against the base of the index finger, and use the tip of the thumb to keep it in place. To pick up food, move the upper chopstick with index and middle fingers. When eating rice and other difficult-to-hold foods, it is better to lift the bowl to the chin and then push the food into the mouth using the chopsticks as a type of shovel, as the Chinese do.

THE ART OF TEA DRINKING

Tea has been known as a drink in China certainly for more than 2,000 years and probably much earlier. However, it was not until the eighth century AD that tea became a common drink, popular with all classes of people. Today, tea drinking is a part of everyday life in China and a pot of strong tea is kept warm all day to provide a regular supply.

When to serve tea

Tea is unlikely to be drunk during the actual meal, as it is generally the custom to place a bowl of clear soup on the table instead for the duration of the meal. Tea is then served at the end of the meal as it is considered to be both refreshing and invigorating.

A Chinese ritual

To the tea connoisseur, tea drinking is almost a mystical ritual. Ideally, preparing tea should be carried out under immaculate and tranquil conditions. The setting is especially important and should be as peaceful as possible; in fact, the ideal spot is considered to be on a mountain so that, as an additional benefit, mountain water is used for the tea. For the connoisseur, the tradition of tea drinking is, as it has always been through the ages, akin to a religious ritual and a return to nature and purity.

DIPPING SAUCES
Traditional sauces for Chinese food include the following:

SWEET & SOUR SAUCE

A tasty sweet and sour sauce which goes well with many deep-fried foods. Store in a well-sealed jar in the refrigerator. It will keep well.

2 tbsp ginger marmalade
2 tbsp orange marmalade
1/4 tsp salt
1 tbsp white rice vinegar (or cider vinegar)
1 tbsp hot water

Combine all the ingredients in a small bowl, mixing well. Serve in a small bowl.

SALT & PEPPER SAUCE

A roasted salt and pepper mixture made with Szechuan peppercorns is found throughout China as a dip for deep-fried foods. The dry-roasting method brings out all the flavors of the peppercorns.

2 oz Szechuan peppercorns
3 oz coarse sea salt

Put a heavy skillet over medium heat. Add the peppercorns and the salt and stir-fry until the mixture begins to brown. Remove the skillet from the heat and let the mixture cool. Grind the mixture in a grinder or with a pestle and mortar.

235

SCALLION SAUCE

Heated oil poured over the seasonings brings out their full flavor. The sauce goes well with meat and poultry dishes.

3 tbsp scallions, chopped finely
3 tbsp fresh gingerroot, grated finely
2 tsp salt
1 tsp light soy sauce
3 tbsp oil (peanut or sunflower)

1. Place the scallions, ginger, salt and soy sauce in a small heatproof bowl.

2. Put the oil into a small saucepan and heat over a moderate heat until it begins to smoke.

3. Remove the oil from the heat and pour over the seasonings. Let the sauce stand for at least 2–3 hours before using, to allow the flavors to blend.

COOKING METHODS

Chinese food generally takes much longer to prepare than it does to cook, so it is very important to prepare each dish as much in advance as possible. Have all the vegetables chopped and sauces blended before you start cooking.

The ingredients should be cut into small, uniformly-sized pieces. This ensures that the food will cook evenly. The prepared food is often cooked very briefly over a high heat, which seals in the natural juices and helps to preserve the nutrients. This short cooking time leaves the end product more succulent and preserves its texture as well as its natural flavors and colors. Shredding vegetables thinly and slicing them diagonally ensures fast cooking, as it increases the area that comes into contact with the hot oil.

Stir-frying

This is the method of cooking most commonly associated with Chinese cuisine. The correct piece of equipment for this is a wok, although any large skillet or heavy saucepan will do. It is best to use a wok (described on page 234) as it gives the best results.

Stir-frying with a wok is a very healthy way to cook, as it uses very little oil and preserves the nutrients in the food as they cook for such a short time. It is very important that the wok is very hot before you begin to cook. This can be tested by holding your hand flat about 3 in over the base of the interior, when you will feel the heat radiating from it. The success of stir-frying lies in having the wok at just the right temperature, and in ensuring correct timing when cooking the food.

Before cooking commences, ensure that all the required ingredients are prepared – chopped, diced and sliced – and so ready to be added to the wok the instant the oil is the right heat. Cooking at too low a temperature or for too long will cause loss of quality.

Add a small amount of oil to the wok and heat it, then add, in stages, the various ingredients to be cooked – those requiring longer cooking go in first, while those that require only very little cooking go in last.

The ingredients should be stirred constantly for a very short time using a long-handled metal or wooden spoon or flat scoop. Constantly stirring ensures that all the ingredients come into contact with the hot oil so the natural juices of the food are sealed in, leaving it crisp and colorful. It also ensures that all the ingredients are evenly cooked. Stir-fried dishes look and taste best when served immediately.

Clean the wok after each use by washing it with water, using a mild detergent if necessary, and a soft cloth or brush. Do not scrub or use any abrasive cleaner as this will scratch the surface. After the washing process is completed, dry the wok thoroughly with paper towels or by placing it over a low heat, then wipe the surface all over with a little oil. This forms a sealing layer to protect the surface of the wok from moisture and thus helps to prevent it from rusting.

Steaming

This is another very popular Chinese method of cooking. The piece of equipment the Chinese use is a bamboo steamer. As these are not airtight, they allow a certain amount of steam to escape, preventing any condensation from forming on the lid. They are designed to stand one on top of another, enabling you to cook several dishes at the same time. Bamboo steamers can be bought at Chinese specialty shops or good cookware shops in a range of sizes.

There are two methods of steaming; in the first the food is arranged on a plate or bowl which is then put inside a steamer on the perforated rack and placed over a large pot of boiling water or put inside a wok. The steam passes through the steamer and cooks the food. Larger items of food such as dumplings can be placed straight on to the rack or laid on cabbage or soaked lotus leaves, which prevents the food from falling through and adds extra flavor. Alternatively, the bowl of ingredients can be immersed partway into the boiling water and the food is cooked partly by the boiling water and partly by the steam it produces.

Deep-frying

Use a wok, a deep-fryer or a heavy-based saucepan. When deep-frying in a wok, use enough oil to give a depth of about 2 inches and heat it over a moderate heat until you can see a faint haze of smoke rising before gently lowering in the food to be fried. Make sure the oil is up to temperature before adding the food: the hot oil should cook the food quickly on the outside, sealing it and forming a barrier around it, which prevents the food from acting like a sponge and becoming soggy and greasy, which is what will happen if the oil is not hot enough.

Before frying the food, ensure that it is dry to prevent the oil from splattering. If the food is in a marinade, let it drain well and, if it is in batter, wait for it to stop dripping. Oil, once it has been strained, can be reused up to three times, but only for the same type of food.

Cook the food in small batches so as not to overcrowd the wok or pan, as this can reduce the temperature of the oil, and lead to unevenly cooked food. Always remove the food from the oil with a perforated spoon and drain on paper towels to absorb any excess oil.

Braising and red braising

This method is similar to Western braising and is generally used with the tougher cuts of meat and the firmer vegetables. The ingredients are stir-fried until lightly brown, stock is added and brought to a boil and then the heat is reduced to simmering until cooking is complete. Red braising uses the same method of cooking but the food is braised in a reddish-brown liquid, such as soy sauce. This sauce can be reused.

Cooking with chopsticks

These long wooden or plastic sticks are not only used for eating but also for cooking, as they are an excellent tool to stir, whip and beat the ingredients during preparation. They can be bought in most cookshops and from many Chinese restaurants.

CHINESE WINE

Chinese wine is mostly made with fermented rice, which gives the wine a very different flavor from wine made with grapes. It is an acquired taste. The best-known Chinese wine is called Shaoxing, which is also used in cooking.

OTHER SUITABLE WINES

Many European and New World wines blend well with Chinese food, particularly the light, dry whites and lighter Burgundy-style reds.

INDEX